KATE ANDERSEN BROWER

The Hill

INSIDE THE
SECRET WORLD
OF THE
U.S. CAPITOL

Quill Tree Books
An Imprint of HarperCollinsPublishers

ALSO BY KATE ANDERSEN BROWER

Exploring the White House:
Inside America's Most Famous Home

Quill Tree Books is an imprint of HarperCollins Publishers.

Library of Congress Control Number: 2023944826
ISBN 978-0-06-322931-0

Typography by Molly Fehr
24 25 26 27 28 LBC 5 4 3 2 1
First Edition

For Teddy

Contents

★ ★ ★

Introduction:

A Hidden City within a City

When you think of the United States Capitol, a vision of the majestic dome that overlooks the sprawling National Mall probably comes to mind. It might just be one of the most famous man-made landmarks in the country. But there is so much more to the Capitol than meets the eye. And while this book isn't trying to be a comprehensive history of change on the Hill, what I hope is that my accounts will inspire you to learn more. So that when you take a closer look, you will see that the Senate and House are separate small "towns," and that the Capitol is like a city itself.

From the moment George Washington laid the cornerstone of the building on September 18, 1793, the Capitol became the most lasting symbol of the hopes, dreams, frustrations, and disappointments of the American people. It's a reflection of who we are. Our country is relatively young—President Joseph Biden's inauguration in January 2021 was only the fifty-ninth ever, and 2026 will mark the country's 250th anniversary. But it is the oldest democracy in the world, and the Capitol is the physical home of the legislative branch of our government—the branch that makes the laws that help this country function.

What are the three branches of government?

The **legislative branch** refers to Congress, the branch of government that makes laws. It is the first branch mentioned in Article I of the Constitution.

The **executive branch** is made up of the president, vice president, cabinet, and most federal agencies that enact the laws passed by Congress. This branch is described in Article II.

The **judicial branch** refers to the Supreme Court and other courts. It is described in Article III.

The Constitution creates these divisions so that one branch will not have any more power than another.

BEHIND THE SCENES

Inside the Capitol, there is a hidden universe. Today, five House office buildings and three Senate office buildings are the offices for 435 representatives and 100 senators. There are an astounding ten thousand staffers as well! The Architect of the Capitol (AOC) is not an architect at all but more like a superintendent or manager for the whole complex, which includes three Library of Congress buildings, the Botanic Garden, the Capitol Visitor Center, the Supreme Court, and the Capitol.

It is essentially its own world! The Capitol even has its own police force of almost two thousand officers, ranking it among the top twenty-five biggest police departments in the United States. There are two subway lines that make it possible to go from one end of the building to the other without ever setting foot outside. And it has its own power plant to keep the lights on, as well as the internet and any other electrical needs.

The famous domed building, located on the eastern end of the National Mall, sits on top of a small hill eighty-eight feet above the Potomac River. From the west front steps, there is a sweeping westward view across the Reflecting Pool to the Washington Monument, 1.4 miles away. The Lincoln Memorial, which is the most visited site on the mall, is 2.2

Aerial view of the National Mall, with the U.S. Capitol in the foreground and the Washington Monument in the distance

miles away. The Capitol building has a central ceremonial rotunda and two separate wings. On either side of the big white dome is the Senate and the House of Representatives, where lawmakers sent to Washington by voters across the country gather to debate national policy and create new laws.

The Capitol complex is more than 1.5 million square feet and has more than six hundred rooms. There are miles and miles of hallways, both aboveground and underground.

There was a longtime deli in the neighborhood, called Roland's, where members of Congress used to grab lunch, and a convenience store nearby. Roland's closed in 2021, but it was a place where members would often run into each other since the 1960s. It was open late at night when a lot of other delis were closed.

> ## DID YOU KNOW?
>
> The Capitol complex has 18.4 million square feet of facilities. And about five million people visit the complex every year!

WHO WORKS IN CONGRESS?

There are a total of 535 members of Congress. Each of the fifty states has two senators who serve six-year terms with no term limits, which means a member of the Senate can be in office as many times as they are reelected. To serve in the Senate, you must be thirty years old and have been a U.S. citizen for at least nine years. The House of Representatives is much larger and has 435 representatives serving districts in each state. Representatives are in office for two years and they also do not face term limits. To be a member of the House, you must be at least twenty-five years old and have been a U.S. citizen for at least seven years.

LEADERSHIP

There are many leaders within both the House of Representatives and the Senate, and each leader has a specific job to help Congress run smoothly. Here are the different titles for the leadership in each group.

★ IN THE HOUSE OF REPRESENTATIVES ★

DID YOU KNOW?

The number of members each state has in the House of Representatives depends on the state's population. For example, Vermont and Delaware have one representative each, while California has more than fifty!

Speaker of the House

After the vice president, the Speaker of the House is the person who is second in line to succeed the president if something were to happen and the president wasn't able to serve. The Speaker is the highest-ranking person in the

House of Representatives, and they decide which legislation comes to the floor.

The Speaker presides over the House, and when they are not available, a Speaker pro tempore fills in. The Speaker oversees the voting schedule in the House Chamber and coordinates the passage of legislation through Congress. They are the head of their party in the House, assign members to select committees, and recruit candidates to run for office. The Speaker has a very full plate!

Majority Leader/Minority Leader

Each party (Democrat or Republican) votes on a member to be their party leader. Since there are an odd number of representatives, the person from the party with the most members in the House is called the majority leader, and the person representing the party with fewer representatives in the House is the minority leader. The majority leader is the second highest-ranking official and manages the daily business of the House. They also communicate the priorities of their specific party, whether that be Democrat or Republican.

The minority leader is the top leader of the minority party in the House (again, that could be Democrat or Republican). They work with their party to create a strategy and to communicate what they want to get done.

Majority Whip/Minority Whip

The majority whip counts the votes and tries to unify their party (Democrat or Republican) behind major issues being discussed. The minority whip does the same, gathering support from the minority party for legislative priorities.

Assistant Speaker/Assistant Democratic Leader

The Assistant Speaker, also known as the Assistant Democratic Leader when the Democratic party is in the minority, was established in 2010 by Nancy Pelosi, who was Speaker of the House at the time. Pelosi created the position to resolve an electoral battle between two Democrats who were vying for the chance to be minority whip. One of them would become minority whip and the other would be named Assistant Democratic Leader when the party was in the minority. It was a way to expand the party's leadership team. When members vote for this position, and some other leaderships posts, it's required that they use an encrypted iPhone, which is given to them by the House. This is done to ensure their votes are kept confidential. They don't have to make it known who they voted for.

Party Caucus Chair

The party caucus chair works to convey the message of the party (Democrat or Republican) to every member and their staff.

★ IN THE SENATE ★

Vice President

The vice president is also the president of the Senate. They are in charge of casting tiebreaking votes and presiding over the counting of electoral ballots cast in presidential elections. They have an office in the Capitol.

President Pro Tempore

The president pro tempore presides over the Senate when the vice president is absent. The term "pro tempore" is Latin, and it means "for the time being," so the president pro tempore is a temporary replacement. The Constitution does not require that it be a member of the Senate, but it always has been throughout history. Since the twentieth century, the longest-serving member of the majority party has usually been elected to the position. They can do everything the vice president can do except cast tiebreaking votes.

Party Leader

Depending on which party is in power (Democrat or Republican), one leader represents the majority and one represents the minority. Party leaders are the spokespeople for what their party stands for. The majority leader schedules which legislation is brought to the floor. The party leaders sit front and center in the Senate Chamber, and they are very involved in what is happening on the Senate floor.

Whip/Majority Whip

Whips are responsible for rounding up votes. Sometimes whips fill in for the majority or minority leaders. They are supposed to "count heads," which means making sure that people in their party are voting the way leadership expects them to.

FUN FACT

The term "whip" comes from fox hunting. "Whipper-in" is a member of a fox hunting team responsible for keeping the dogs from getting distracted and running away during a chase.

THE STAFF

Just like the staff at the White House, who devote their careers to creating a sense of privacy for the first family, the Capitol Hill staff work very hard to provide a place to escape for members of Congress.

But in addition to those who work within the Capitol, there is also a tremendous amount of upkeep that goes into maintaining the building. The people who work behind the scenes to take care of the Capitol building and its grounds are dedicated to preserving and maintaining the historic buildings that fall under the purview of the Architect of the Capitol. More than two thousand people work for the AOC in jobs that include groundskeepers and engineers. Since 1793, the AOC has maintained the 18.4 million square feet of facilities, including the Supreme Court and the Library of Congress, thousands of works of art, and 570 acres of grounds. And sometimes, the job of keeping the Capitol maintained is a dirty one. For example, so many bird droppings land on the massive complex that every spring and fall, the Washington fire department comes to hose it down. And every four years, the building is painted, which means that on some of the oldest sections of the Capitol, there are dozens and dozens of coats of paint!

Many immigrants from all over the world have served on the Hill in different jobs. The United States is a nation of immigrants, a country that has sought to embody the inspirational words written on the Statue of Liberty by poet and activist Emma Lazarus: "Give me your tired, your poor, your huddled masses yearning to breathe free." And to the people who work on Capitol Hill, there is nothing more important than keeping it looking as majestic as it did when it was first built.

FINAL THOUGHTS

This book will shine a light on one of the country's most important buildings and all the people who dedicate their lives to working in and maintaining it. For this is not only a job to them but also a role in preserving our democracy. Many of them have traveled a long way in order to be part of this country's profound history.

★ ★ ★

PLACES

★ ★ ★

Where It All Began . . .

After the Revolutionary War, which was fought from 1775 to 1783, when the United States won independence from Great Britain, the business of setting up a new kind of government was at hand. In 1776, John Adams, who later became the country's second president, wrote in his essay "Thoughts on Government":

> As good government, is an empire of laws, how shall your laws be made? In a large society, inhabiting an extensive country, it is impossible that the whole should assemble, to make laws: The first necessary step then, is, to depute power from the many, to a few of the most wise and good.

Essentially, John Adams was saying that the government needs a small number of representatives for the many citizens of the United States. Members of Congress are voted into office by the people, and their job is to represent the interests of the people in their state, not just those who voted for them.

And for a law to be passed, members of the House and the Senate must agree. In order to get legislation enacted, senators and representatives must learn to compromise. Without that, nothing can be accomplished. Many people complain about

DID YOU KNOW?

Congress was established by the Constitution, and the First Congress met between 1789 and 1791. Before the Constitution was ratified in 1788, however, the Continental Congress and the Congress of the Confederation, acting as the effective national government during the Revolution, met in various places, including Annapolis, Maryland; and Trenton, New Jersey. Once the Constitution was officially accepted as the written charter of government, representatives gathered in New York City's Federal Hall, and how long it takes for things to get done, but compromise can be very difficult.

So, in the late 1700s, a decision needed to be made. Where should the center of democracy sit? But exactly where the capital city should be located was a hot topic among the founding fathers. There was fierce competition between Philadelphia and New York, but in the end, Washington, D.C., won out.

then they moved to Congress Hall in Philadelphia. Congress's first two years were especially important. Members were establishing the new system of a democratic republic, where voters (at the time the right to vote was severely restricted and only wealthy white men who owned property had any power) decide on issues through their elected representatives. The first Congress passed the Bill of Rights and inaugurated the first president. Congress met in Philadelphia's Congress Hall from 1790 to 1800 and then they moved to the newly built Capitol in Washington, D.C.

★ ★ ★

DIFFERENT LOCATIONS
FOR THE CAPITAL, 1781–1800

March 1, 1781, to June 21, 1783:
Philadelphia, Pennsylvania—State House
(now Independence Hall)

June 30, 1783, to November 4, 1783:
Princeton, New Jersey—Nassau Hall

November 26, 1783, to August 19, 1784:
Annapolis, Maryland—State House

November 1, 1784, to December 24, 1784:
Trenton, New Jersey—French Arms Tavern

January 11, 1785, to Autumn 1788:
New York, New York—Fraunces Tavern

March 4, 1789, to August 12, 1790:
New York, New York—Federal Hall

December 6, 1790, to May 14, 1800:
Philadelphia, Pennsylvania—Congress Hall

November 17, 1800:
Washington, D.C.—U.S. Capitol

The path to choose Washington, D.C., as the capital seems inevitable now. It was clear that where it sits on the map had a lot of things going for it. Unlike Philadelphia and New York, Washington's exact location was handpicked by President George Washington. It was close to his Mount Vernon home, and it was also in the middle of the east coast of the country, with easy access to the Potomac and the Anacostia Rivers. It was a convenient trading hub and easy to defend.

George Washington understood the importance of selecting a place that would unite the North and the South, as well as the East and the West. He was elected president in 1789 (though the election was far from inclusive, since he was unanimously elected with only sixty-nine electoral votes, long before the rules of modern-day elections were established), and he had to decide how the presidency should work. There were no examples to follow—George Washington was the first! "I walk on untrodden ground," he often said.

Then, in 1790, Washington, D.C., was officially established by Congress, who enacted the Residence Act. Although it seemed to be an ideal place, there were downsides too. It was muggy, undeveloped swampland. So, Philadelphia was set up as the temporary capital while Washington was being built from the ground up.

THE CAPITOL DESIGN

Once the location was decided, the first architect was hired to design the Capitol. But he was not even a trained architect! So how was he chosen?

President George Washington and his secretary of state, Thomas Jefferson, hatched an innovative plan: they created a competition for the best design for the Capitol complex. The winner of the competition would receive $500, an enormous amount of money at the time, and the second-place winner would take home $250. Washington and Jefferson had some specific requirements as well: the complex should be made of brick and must have plenty of space, including a conference room and a room for representatives, with both rooms able to hold three hundred people each; a lobby; a Senate room with its own lobby; and twelve smaller committee rooms.

In 1792, advertisements detailing the search were placed in the newspaper, making it the first government-sponsored competition of its kind.

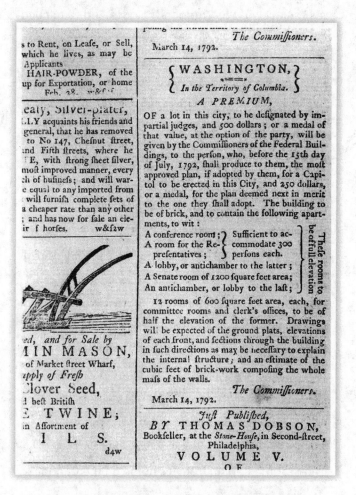

Announcement of Capitol Design Competition. Dunlap's American Daily Advertiser (Philadelphia), March 24, 1792.

DID YOU KNOW?

A similar contest to design the White House (which was then called the President's House) led to a much quicker decision. Irish-born James Hoban's design won easily. The Capitol was a longer process because there were a lot of people to accommodate, and no designs won out immediately. The Capitol building would have to be incredible. The structure needed to be both a landmark in the new capital city as well as a symbol of democracy along the banks of the Potomac River. It was going to be the centerpiece of the city and the physical embodiment of America and its new form of government. The founders wanted it to rival the beauty of European capitals. Washington and Jefferson were disappointed with the early entries until they came upon one from more than a thousand miles away, designed by someone with no formal architectural training. On top of that, the plans were submitted six months past deadline! In 1792, William Thornton was a thirty-three-year-old doctor exploring his passion for architecture when he decided to sketch his vision for the Capitol from his home on the Caribbean island of Tortola.

William Thornton, 1804

DID YOU KNOW?

Tortola is now part of the British Virgin Islands. When Thornton was growing up as the son of wealthy planters, he saw that his family fortune was made by enslaving people to grow indigo, tobacco, cotton, and sugar on the twelve-mile-long island. Thornton tried without success to convince his family to release the enslaved people working on the plantation.

Thornton's neoclassical design was inspired by Greek and Roman architecture, and it was massive. Three and a half times larger than Philadelphia's Independence Hall! Washington loved the grand yet simple design with a domed rotunda in the center flanked by wings for the Senate and the House of Representatives. It was as majestic as any government building in Paris or London—those who doubted whether democracy could survive would now be in awe of the grand building that would become its symbol.

Washington, Jefferson, and the commissioners selected to survey the site and oversee the building's design accepted Thornton's plans in 1793, and he received the $500 prize. In 1788, Thornton became an American citizen, and shortly after that he moved to Washington. George Washington laid the cornerstone of the Capitol as ceremonial guns were fired in celebration. A local newspaper described the theatrical ceremony, which included "music playing, drums beating, colors flying, and spectators rejoicing." The new country finally had its seat of government.

DID YOU KNOW?

The spot where the Capitol was built was called Jenkins Hill before Jefferson coined the name "Capitol Hill," after ancient Rome's Capitoline Hill, which housed the Jupiter Optimus Maximus temple. George Washington was good friends with Pierre Charles L'Enfant, a Frenchman who had left his country to come to America to fight in the Revolutionary War. Washington appointed him to design the city of Washington, D.C. But L'Enfant's vision of grand avenues and public squares, designed using a grid system of wide boulevards named after states, similar to his home city of Paris, took a lot of time to be realized. As L'Enfant said, the "wilderness" (referring to the swamp-like land) must be transformed into a city befitting the hopeful and vast new country. L'Enfant called the subtle slope, which is about eighty feet high in the center of Washington, D.C., "a pedestal waiting for a monument."

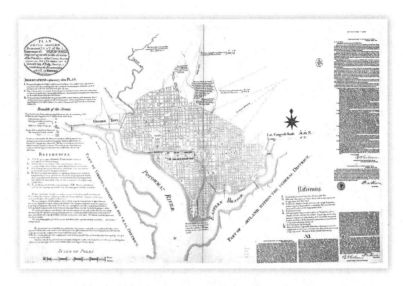

Facsimile of 1791 L'Enfant Plan of Washington from national archives

DID YOU KNOW?

George Washington was the only president inaugurated in two cities—and Washington, D.C., was not one of them! He was first inaugurated in New York City at Federal Hall in 1789, and his second inauguration, in 1793, was held in Philadelphia's Congress Hall.

The unfinished Capitol, June 28, 1863

WHO BUILT THE CAPITOL?

There is no way to tell the story of the building of the Capitol without recognizing the people who were forced to build it. The Capitol is a symbol of liberty—of freedom—for many Americans, but it was actually built by enslaved people who were deprived of the most basic liberties the building represented. The federal government paid plantation owners to use their enslaved workers, and the enslavers kept the money. The government provided housing and food rations for all the laborers. The hypocrisy of enslaving people to build a symbol of freedom infuriated abolitionists. Julian Niemcewicz, a Polish writer who visited Washington, D.C., in the 1790s, was overcome with sadness by what he saw:

> *I have seen [slaves] in large numbers and I was very glad that these poor unfortunates earned eight to ten dollars per week. My joy was not long lived: I am told that they were not working for themselves; their masters hire them out and retain all the money for themselves. What humanity! What a country of liberty.*

Construction began in August 1793, and although Thornton said that he was against slavery, it was enslaved people and free laborers who brought his design to life. It is unknown whether he voiced disapproval.

At least two hundred known enslaved laborers built the Capitol and the nearby White House. They did the backbreaking work of excavating the Aquia Creek sandstone from a Virginia quarry, which was then used for the exterior facade and interior design of the Capitol. The sandstone was so heavy that it had to be brought up the Potomac River to the Capitol by ferry. Enslaved laborers worked as carpenters and painters, and their work was exhausting, lasting six days a week and requiring knowledge and skill. They worked through the searing heat and humid summers and bitter-cold winters of Washington, D.C. They slept in huts near the construction site and many of them got sick.

DID YOU KNOW?

Philip Reid was an enslaved man who was a sculptor's apprentice. Reid had been born into slavery and purchased in Charleston, South Carolina, for $700. He worked on the bronze *Statue of Freedom* sculpture that sits at the top of the Capitol dome. The nineteen-and-a-half-foot statue of a woman arrived in a fifteen-thousand-pound plaster cast from Italy. Reid was key to the process of casting it in bronze because he figured out a way to disassemble the plaster model so that it could be moved from the Capitol to a workshop where it could be cast in bronze.

Slavery was abolished in Washington, D.C., on April 16, 1862. Reid was forty-two years old when he could finally be free, though there were still legal limitations on his freedom, including not having the right to vote. A year later, the *Statue of Freedom* was unveiled on top of the dome.

In 2012, the Capitol Visitor Center added a marker in Emancipation Hall with a block of Aquia Creek sandstone and the following message, which pays tribute to the enslaved laborers: "This sandstone was originally part of the United States Capitol's East Front, constructed in 1824–1826. It was quarried by laborers including enslaved African Americans and commemorates their important role in building the Capitol."

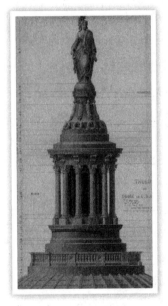

Statue of Freedom

Marker commemorating enslaved laborers

DID YOU KNOW?

On August 24, 1814, during the War of 1812, the British marched into Washington and set fire to the Capitol building. The British chose to invade Washington because of its symbolic importance, its easy access from the sea, and the inexperienced American troops attempting to defend it. A painting by Paul de Rapin depicts this:

WHAT ABOUT THE COURTS?

Even once Congress was officially meeting in Washington, other major parts of the government were in a state of flux. In addition to the House and the Senate, the third branch of the government, the judicial branch, was also housed in the Capitol complex, until the court received its own building in 1935. There was no provision made for a Supreme Court building, and within the Capitol, the location changed a half dozen times! Between 1801 and 1809, justices met in a modest committee room. From 1810 until 1860, they met in a grander semicircular room with vaulted ceilings now known as the Old Supreme Court Chamber. In 1860, they had to move upstairs into yet another room in the Senate.

Old Supreme Court Chamber

Then, in 1935, the Supreme Court finally got its own building, an incredible 146 years after it began. The Old Supreme Court Chamber inside the Capitol was not treated with much respect; it actually sat vacant in the 1960s up until 1975, when it was finally restored.

FUN FACT

Before the Supreme Court justices moved into the Capitol, they met wherever the U.S. Capitol happened to be at the time, from the Merchants Exchange Building in New York City to Independence Hall in Philadelphia.

DID YOU KNOW?

The Capitol served as a hospital during the Civil War. On August 31, 1862, the headquarters of the Military District of Washington issued Special Order 177, turning the Capitol into a hospital after a battle. The Union had suffered 16,000 causalities and needed somewhere to take care of injured Union soldiers. If you had walked through the Rotunda, you would have seen hundreds of soldiers; it is estimated between 1,100 and 1,200 sick and wounded soldiers were brought to the Capitol during the Civil War.

Rotunda during the Civil War, 1862

WHAT MAKES UP THE CAPITOL COMPLEX TODAY?

The Capitol has grown in size and stature as the United States has flourished. Today, it is more than 1.5 million square feet, it has more than six hundred rooms, and it has many miles of hallways. It has five levels. The first floor has mostly committee rooms and space for congressional officers. The second floor has what we have come to know the Capitol for: chambers of the House of Representatives and the Senate in addition to Congress's offices. In the center is the Rotunda. The third floor has offices and press spaces as well as a gallery where visitors can watch the House and the Senate when they are in session. Finally, the fourth floor and the basement are mostly offices and other facilities' areas.

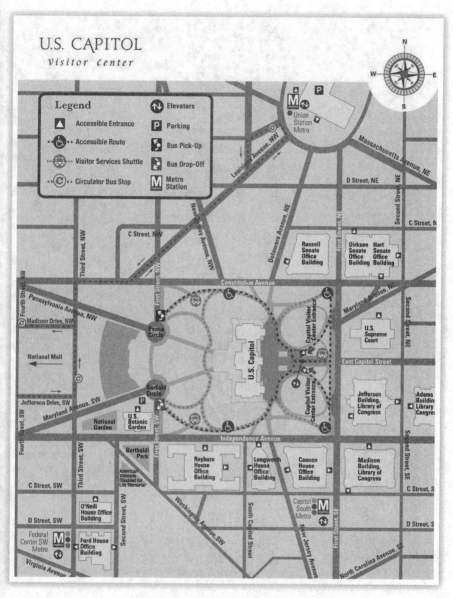

U.S. Capitol map from the Visitor Center

U.S. CAPITOL MAP

1. Russell Senate Office Building
2. Dirksen Senate Office Building
3. Hart Senate Office Building
4. Supreme Court of the United States
5. Jefferson Building: Library of Congress
6. Adams Building: Library of Congress
7. Madison Building: Library of Congress
8. Cannon House Office Building
9. Longworth House Office Building
10. Rayburn House Office Building
11. Ford House Office Building
12. O'Neill House Office Building
13. U.S. Botanic Garden
14. Capitol Visitor Center

Map of the Capitol campus

37

* ★ *

The Rotunda

One of the most symbolic parts of the Capitol complex is its 8.9-million-pound, 288-foot-tall cast-iron dome called the Rotunda. The Rotunda area is used for important events, like dedicating works of art or the lying in state of important political figures.

The Rotunda was not built at the time of the other parts of the Capitol complex due to lack of funds as well as a shortage of materials. When the British burned the Capitol during the War of 1812, the Rotunda's construction was delayed; it wasn't finished until 1824. Over the years, there has been work done on the Rotunda. It was last restored over the course of more than twenty-five years, between 1990 and 2017. The position of Architect of the Capitol—the person in charge of preserving and caring for the massive facilities, thousands of works of art, and hundreds of acres—is held for a ten-year term, so the project began with the ninth Architect of the Capitol and was continued by the tenth. The restoration was finally completed by the eleventh Architect of the Capitol, but it will need to be restored again and again.

Capitol Rotunda

DID YOU KNOW?

Government officials or military officers "lie in state" and private citizens "lie in honor." After they pass away, their bodies are brought to the Rotunda and members of the public can come and pay their respects. Supreme Court justice Ruth Bader Ginsburg was the first woman to lie in state at the U.S. Capitol when she passed away in 2020. More than thirty-four men, including President Abraham Lincoln and Senator John McCain, were also given that high honor.

DID YOU KNOW?

At a House Appropriations Committee hearing to fund the most recent restoration, the architect at the time brought in a Maxwell House coffee can filled with ten pounds of rust from the dome. It was his evidence that funding was desperately needed.

FUN FACT

After a restoration project and three coats of paint—that's 1,215 gallons!—the Capitol dome was revealed in 2016 after three years of being covered in scaffolding. The topcoat was actually called "dome white."

★ ★ ★

MARRIAGE AT THE CAPITOL

There have been many marriages at the Capitol, some because the couple simply loved the symbol of American democracy and others that were political statements. Some members of Congress have even gotten married on Capitol Hill, which to them is like having a wedding at the office.

A 1902 *New York Times* headline read: "Married on Capitol Dome: Young Couple Made Man and Wife 375 Feet Above Ground at Washington." The groom, Andres Diaz y Pairo of Cuba, and the bride, Catherine McConochie of Canada, met in New York and decided to be married at the dome. Shortly before 1:00 p.m., they climbed to the top, hand in hand. They were accompanied by two police officers, two newspaper reporters, and a justice of the peace to marry them. It is remarkable that neither of them were U.S. citizens; they simply thought the Capitol was beautiful.

It is also incredible that no one stopped them, and that the police officers with them served as their escorts. There was a statute that said no marriage could take place at the Capitol unless the Speaker of the House and the president of the Senate gave their consent. Sergeant-at-Arms Ransdell of the Senate tried to stop the marriage, but he was too late.

After they were wed, they took out their camera and began snapping photographs of each other and their unusual wedding venue. A crowd gathered at the stairway leading to the dome and on the steps outside. The couple were escorted into a carriage that took them to the train station to travel to New York, where they boarded a ship to Europe for their honeymoon. They eventually settled in Havana, Cuba. In 1944, an Arkansas couple married in the subcommittee room of Senator Hattie Caraway, the first woman elected to serve a full term in the Senate. Caraway was the matron of honor, and Arkansas representative William Fadjo Cravens conducted the ceremony.

Sometimes marriages inside the Capitol were meant to send a political message. One such marriage took place during the Cold War, the period after World War II when the United States and the Soviet Union (now Russia) were locked in a nuclear stalemate, each possessing weapons that could destroy the other's country. In May 1982, Edward Lozansky, a twenty-nine-year-old Soviet immigrant, remarried a Soviet general's daughter who had started a hunger strike so that she could leave Moscow. It was a very unusual ceremony because the bride could not be there. The ceremony took place in a small room at the U.S. Capitol, and the Reform Jewish wedding was witnessed by Senator Bob Dole, a Republican from Kansas, and the best man was Representative Jack Kemp, a Republican from New York. The bride, Tatyana Lozansky, also twenty-nine years old, was using the hunger strike to put pressure on her government. A woman whose husband was among the hunger strikers stood in for Tatyana at the wedding.

Rabbi Joshua Haberman, a leader of Washington's oldest and largest synagogue, performed the ceremony in Hebrew and English and noted that the wedding was being held in "the very center of the Free World." The room was precisely between the Senate and the House Chambers, directly in the middle of the Capitol.

It is far less controversial for actual members of Congress to marry in the Capitol. They have long been taking advantage of their unique office space and transforming it into a wedding venue. There was a period in the 1990s when there was an average of one wedding a year in the Capitol. On Valentine's Day in 1996, Republican Senator Bill Cohen of Maine married Janet Langhart in the Mike Mansfield Room, named after the longest-serving Senate majority leader. They needed the big space to accommodate one hundred guests, who were entertained by musicians playing classical music on a violin, viola, and cello. "It's very sweet and very romantic," one guest said.

But members of Congress usually marry in the chapel, also known as the prayer room, near the Rotunda. It was created in the 1950s. Because of the separation of church and state, it is not overtly religious; it is a peaceful place for reflection for members of Congress. The room, which seats just ten people, has a stained-glass window with an image of George Washington kneeling in prayer. He is surrounded by the words from Psalms 16:1 "Preserve me, O God; For in Thee do I put my trust." The chapel is not open to the public.

The House Chamber

Inside the House Chamber, many historic events have taken place that reflect the changes in American society.

The House Chamber has moved locations and has been through many renovations over the past two centuries. When the British set fire to the Capitol in 1814, they destroyed the first chamber. It reopened in 1819 in what is now Statuary Hall. The Old House Chamber looked like a Greek theater. It was not user-friendly because it was awkward for members to even turn their chairs around to look at people speaking to them.

The House met in what we know as the House Chamber for the first time on December 16, 1857. At that time, there were 234 representatives from thirty-two states and seven

Prayer at meeting of House of Representatives,
interior of chamber, Washington, D.C.

territories, and they each sat at separate desks. In the 1850s, the chamber was each member's office, because they had nowhere else to go. Today, members sit on benches and can sit wherever they want; however, Democrats usually sit on the left side of the aisle and Republicans sit on the right side. Because of this, Democrats are often referred to as the political "left" and Republicans are the political "right."

Three House office buildings are on Independence Avenue just south of the Capitol. The Rayburn House Office building is the only one with a train connecting it to the Capitol. The Cannon and Longworth buildings are closer to the Capitol and are connected by underground tunnels. Most members of Congress want to be in the 2.4-million-square-foot Rayburn building because it's the newest (it was built in 1965) and it has that underground train that makes going to and from the Capitol to vote much easier.

The Ford Building is named after Gerald R. Ford, a longtime Michigan congressman who went on to serve as vice president and then president in the 1970s. It's a few blocks from the Capitol in an area known as Federal Center SW.

The O'Neill Building is named after Thomas "Tip" O'Neill Jr., a Massachusetts Democrat who was Speaker of the House from 1977 to 1987.

DID YOU KNOW?

Each time a member of Congress is defeated, retires, or passes away, their office becomes available to the most senior member waiting for an upgrade, be it to an office with more space or one with a better view. The Architect of the Capitol handles the reshuffling.

In the Senate, it all depends on seniority. For freshman senators, their experience in government and how many people live in their state is taken into account. If you were a Cabinet secretary or in the House, you are guaranteed a nicer office than someone who has never worked in the federal government before.

The House Chamber is located in the Capitol's south wing. It was originally designed with no windows so that members wouldn't be distracted by noise or any sort of interference. Before it was remodeled in 1949 and 1950, when the white marble was replaced with walnut wood, natural light came in from the ceiling, where there was a large skylight. But the skylight was a Victorian era addition, and it was eventually removed. Now there is an eagle with its wings spread wide-open that looks almost like stained glass. An artificial light shines through it to help illuminate the chamber.

You can visit the House Chamber and sit upstairs. You might be able to make out these words on a plaque on a wall high up above the Speaker's rostrum. They are from Massachusetts representative and senator Daniel Webster, and were delivered in 1825. They are there to inspire and remind members of Congress of their duty: "Let us develop the resources of our land, call forth its powers, build up its institutions, promote all its great interests and see whether we also, in our day and generation, may not perform something worthy to be remembered."

There are also portraits of the French general Marquis de Lafayette and George Washington in the House Chamber. Lafayette, being a close friend and an ally of Washington's, was the first foreign dignitary ever to speak in the chamber. It was actually Lafayette's portrait that was commissioned first, and afterward, a portrait of Washington was made.

The phrase "In God We Trust" was added above the rostrum on December 19, 1962, when the United States and the Soviet Union were locked in the Cold War. The Soviet Union's leaders discouraged any religious beliefs, and the addition of the phrase highlighted the difference between the United States, where there is freedom of religion, and the Soviet Union.

★★★

WHAT IS THE ROSTRUM
AND WHAT HAPPENS THERE?

The rostrum is the raised platform where the Speaker of the House guides legislative business. The presiding officer and parliamentarians keep legislative business moving. The clerk

House rostrum

of the House's staff announces the business before the House, and they run the voting schedule.

A dictionary always lies open next to the rostrum in case a word needs to be double-checked. The rostrum itself is made of beautiful walnut with laurel branches carved into it. It was originally smaller and made of white marble, but today, it is much larger to accommodate more people, and

the wood is warmer than the cold white marble. A silver inkstand sits in front of the Speaker before every session; it is the oldest artifact in the House.

DID YOU KNOW?

When the president of the United States addresses Congress, he speaks in the House Chamber, and depending on when he speaks, it is either referred to as remarks delivered before a joint session of Congress or the State of the Union. The difference is only timing! If the president speaks shortly after his inaugural address, then that first speech is before a joint session of Congress.

The Constitution requires that the president "shall from time to time give to the Congress Information of the State of the Union, and recommend to their Consideration such Measures as he shall judge necessary and expedient." But, it reasoned, the president would not know enough about the "State of the Union" until he has been in office for at least a year.

The Speaker's Lobby, an elegant space with ceilings painted in gold, can be entered through the doors on either side of the rostrum. When Congress is in session, members can go there and discuss laws that are up for debate in private. It is also where they can work to convince people to come to their side. In the nineteenth century, when members did not have their own offices, the public could visit them here to discuss causes or bills they cared about. That is where the term "lobbying" is thought to have come from. Now, most people are not allowed inside.

Portraits of the speakers of the House of Representatives line the walls of the Speaker's Lobby just outside the House Chamber at the U.S. Capitol.

★ ★ ★

SOME EARLY FIRSTS

The First Woman Who Spoke before the House

When the House and Senate Chambers were being built, members sometimes met in the much smaller Library of Congress's reading room. It was here on January 12, 1806, that Dorothy Ripley delivered a sermon. It was a Sunday during a time when there were few large spaces to speak, and the temporary House Chamber was sometimes used as a place of worship. Thomas Jefferson, who was the nation's third president, was in attendance to hear her speak.

The First Black Person Who Spoke in the House Chamber

It was not until February 12, 1865, that a Black man spoke in the House Chamber. Like Dorothy Ripley, Henry Highland Garnet was a preacher. He had been invited by the House chaplain to speak in celebration of the House's approval of the Thirteenth Amendment, which abolished slavery. Garnet was born enslaved. Black people had been kept from the House and Senate Chambers, and now here was Garnet, a preacher at a nearby Washington Presbyterian church, speaking about the evils and horrors of slavery. Garnet called upon Congress to do its job to "Emancipate, Enfranchise, [and to] Educate" the men and women who had been enslaved. Of slavery, he said, "Upon the total and complete destruction of this accursed sin depends the safety and perpetuity of our Republic and its excellent institutions."

VOTING IN THE HOUSE OF REPRESENTATIVES

Voting in the House of Representatives started off simply, with debate and declaration of opinion. But in 1888, the House approved legislation to install signal bells in the House wing of the Capitol so that representatives would know what was happening in the House Chamber when they were in their offices. It wasn't until 1908, when the first House office building was opened, that they were put in place. Bells—and later lights—are still used as a way of letting members of Congress know what is happening on the House floor.

THE FIRST ELECTRONIC VOTE

Electronic voting did not become standard until 1973. Before then, there was a handheld counter that party leaders used to register votes. It has been estimated that electronic voting saves more than ninety hours of work every year because it makes the process so much faster.

But much of what happens on the Hill is done because it is part of long-standing tradition. For instance, there is a "bill hopper," where representatives actually introduce bills by placing them in the hopper. The "hopper" is a reference to bins used on farms to store grains. Someone collects the bills in the hopper and refers them to the appropriate committees, where they are then considered.

The U.S. House bill hopper

★ ★ ★

HOW DOES A BILL MOVE THROUGH CONGRESS AND LAND ON THE PRESIDENT'S DESK?

The House of Representatives comes up with and passes legislation, which usually is created through bills—essentially laws in progress. Once the House, Senate, and president are in agreement, the bill becomes a law.

Members introduce thousands of bills each year. First, a representative places the bill in the hopper on the Speaker's rostrum. Then times are scheduled in the House to debate the bill, and representatives go to the lectern at the front of the chamber to make their case for or against the bill. Each minute is accounted for by the Rules Committee, which decides how much time each major bill gets on the floor.

When it is time for representatives to leave their offices and vote on legislation, a signal clock buzzes and flashes all around the Capitol campus, telling them that it's time to go and cast their vote.

★ ★ ★

The Senate Chamber

Unlike the House Chamber, the Senate Chamber has individual desks where one hundred senators sit on a semicircular platform in front of a rostrum, similar to the one in the House. And much like the House, the leaders of the Senate sit behind the rostrum to preside over the Senate.

The new Senate Chamber

From 1819 until 1859, senators met in a different room in the Capitol's north wing, near the Rotunda. This is one of the oldest rooms in the entire Capitol, and it is elaborately decorated, with a half dome and marble columns. This room was also home to the Supreme Court from 1860 to 1935 and is known as the Old Senate Chamber. It was restored in 1976 and is now a museum.

The Old Senate Chamber

Above the red fabric canopy is a portrait of George Washington, purchased in 1832. The desk in the center of the room was reserved for the vice president, who is also president of the Senate. In front of the vice president's desk is a larger desk for the secretary of the Senate and the chief clerk. People once gathered in the gallery to watch debates, many of them revolving around slavery, which was the most important issue of the time.

The one hundred desks in the Senate Chamber are among the most recognizable symbols of the Senate. When the British set fire to the U.S. Capitol in 1814, the Senate Chamber (now the Old Senate Chamber) was almost completely destroyed. As part of the reconstruction plan, the Senate hired New York cabinetmaker Thomas Constantine to build forty-eight desks and chairs. When the chamber was restored in 1819, each senator had his own desk. There were only forty-eight senators at the time because there were not yet fifty states. As each new state became part of the Union, new desks were built to accommodate the new senators.

In 1859, when the Senate moved into their current chamber, the desks came along with the senators. Up until 1877, each desk was made by private cabinetmakers. Since 1877, however, new desks have been built by the cabinet shop in the basement of the Capitol. Around 1959, the most recent six desks were built: two new senators from Alaska, two new senators from Hawaii, and two replacement desks.

Each one of the one hundred desks has a unique shape, depending on where it was placed in the original Old Senate Chamber. For instance, aisle desks were narrow and angled, compared to wider desks that were at the center. Now senators choose which desk they sit at and where they sit in the chamber. It is a fairly recent tradition for senators to write their names inside the desk drawers. The earliest names were signed in the first decade of the 1900s. In some cases, staff members wrote the names, but more recently, senators have signed their own names; they are proud to be part of this tradition.

Which desk belonged to which senator used to be kept a secret. It was believed that people might try to steal the desks of famous senators, like Henry Clay or Daniel Webster. Chairs are a different story. Though there has been a great effort to preserve the history of the Senate, only three of the original 1819 chairs are known to exist. Now senators leaving office can buy their chairs, and chairs are made to replace them after every election, which keeps the furniture makers busy.

Though tradition is important in the Senate, it has changed with the times. The rules of the Senate do not allow "the taking of pictures of any kind" inside the Senate Chamber. On September 24, 1963,

U.S. Senate in session, September 1963

the Senate made an exception so that the first official photograph could be taken.

Today, the Senate's own photographic studio takes the official photo for each two-year Congress.

TELEVISION IN THE CHAMBER

When the House of Representatives allowed its sessions to be broadcast live in 1979 by C-SPAN (the Cable-Satellite Public Affairs Network), senators did not want the same thing to happen in their chamber. But in 1986, Senate leaders Robert Dole and Robert Byrd proposed the idea of live coverage of the Senate session, and C-SPAN 2 began broadcasting them. Now anyone can watch the Senate in action.

Senator Robert Dole of Kansas (1969–1996) during the first live television broadcast from the Senate Chamber

Even though a lot has not changed, the Senate does make use of new technology. But senators still sit at the same desks and listen to similarly spirited debates, albeit regarding different topics, as their predecessors did in the nineteenth century.

★ ★ ★

SENATE FIRSTS . . .

In 1861, Mississippi senator Jefferson Davis led a group of Southern senators out of the chamber in an early sign that the South was leaving the Union. Davis went on to lead the Confederacy. In 1870, Senator Hiram Revels became the first Black member of Congress. And in 1922, Rebecca Felton became the Senate's first female member, though she served for only one day and was known to be a white supremacist.

On May 16, 1991, the late Queen Elizabeth II became the first religious leader to address a joint meeting of Congress. We think of her as the queen of England, but she was also the head of the Anglican Church. When she was in Washington, D.C., she wanted to see America's favorite pastime, and so she went to a baseball game between the Baltimore Orioles and Oakland Athletics.

With Speaker Tom Foley (right) and Vice President Dan Quayle (left) in the background, Queen Elizabeth II of the United Kingdom gives a speech to Congress.

... AND NOTABLE SPEAKERS

When foreign dignitaries visit Congress, they usually speak in the House Chamber because it's bigger. But when British prime minister Winston Churchill came to the United States on December 26, 1941, less than three weeks after the nation entered the Second World War, he spoke in the Senate Chamber. Because it was the day after Christmas, most members were out of town, but the chamber was packed. Additional chairs had to be set up at the back of the room. As Churchill spoke, people cheered and made V-for-victory signs with their fingers.

The prime minister made the audience laugh, even during a dark time in history. "The fact . . . that here I am, an Englishman, welcomed in your midst, makes this experience one of the most moving and thrilling in my life," he said, "which is already long and has not been entirely uneventful." The audience laughed, but then Churchill got serious when he described the end goal of the Axis powers, which were made up of Germany, Italy, and Japan. He said they are "enormous; they are bitter; they are ruthless." He called them "wicked men," and he said they must "know they will be called to terrible account."

Churchill addressed joint meetings of Congress two more times, in 1943 and 1952. Churchill and Israeli prime minister

Benjamin Netanyahu share the distinction of having made more addresses to Congress than any other foreign leaders. In recent years, Ukrainian president Volodymyr Zelensky has addressed Congress seeking American aid and support against the Russian invasion of his country.

DID YOU KNOW?

Though it is not in the Constitution, the filibuster is a tradition of the Senate that allows senators to give long speeches to delay action on a resolution, bill, or amendment during the Senate session. In 1917, the Senate adopted a rule known as "cloture," so that a two-thirds majority can put an end to a filibuster. In 1975, the Senate lowered the votes needed for cloture to sixty of the one-hundred-member Senate. There is an ongoing debate whether to end the filibuster completely. Critics say it is a tool of obstruction that allows the minority to block the majority from acting on policies.

The longest filibuster was a speech given by Senator Strom Thurmond of South Carolina. He spoke for twenty-four hours and eighteen minutes against the Civil Rights Act of 1957. The landmark bill eventually passed, despite Thurmond's wishes. Senators have used the filibuster more often in the past couple of decades as partisanship—the political divide between Republicans and Democrats—has become wider. Those in favor of continuing the filibuster say that because we live in a democratic republic, the filibuster serves to keep the Senate a place for free speech and meaningful debate.

WHEN CONGRESS INVESTIGATES

The Constitution outlined three essential powers of Congress: the power to determine the budget, the power to declare war, and the power to launch investigations.

During investigative hearings, senators question witnesses, much like in a court system, and sometimes they uncover terrible secrets and reveal wrongdoing. It is essential to democracy that this process exists, even though hearings sometimes happen that never should have in the first place. One famous example of this is the 1954 Army–McCarthy Hearings. This happened during a time called the Red Scare, when the U.S. government was worried about Communism spreading from the Soviet Union throughout the United States during the Cold War. Wisconsin senator Joseph McCarthy claimed that hundreds of Communists were working in the U.S. State Department. McCarthy held hearings, calling in members of the government and Hollywood celebrities and producers and accusing them of being Communists. He ruined people's careers, often without strong evidence, by accusing them of having ties to the Communist Party.

The nationally televised hearings exposed how reckless McCarthy could be. Eventually his fellow senators voted to censure him, which meant he no longer had the power and prestige he once had. Censuring is much less severe than actually forcing someone to leave Congress. But it was clear that after being censured, McCarthy had lost the respect of his Senate colleagues, and he was therefore much less powerful.

Two decades after McCarthy was censured, the Senate held a hearing to investigate the Watergate scandal in 1973. The Senate Select Committee on Presidential Campaign Activities—known as the Watergate Committee— investigated "illegal, improper, or unethical activities" related to the 1972 presidential race between the sitting president, Richard Nixon, and George McGovern. They investigated claims that Nixon campaign aides had broken into the headquarters of the Democratic National Committee (DNC) at the Watergate Hotel, which led to Nixon's resignation. It is the first and only time that a president has ever resigned.

DID YOU KNOW?

Members of the House are in a powerful position because they can hold legislative and investigative hearings. Witnesses testify in legislative hearings to guide the direction of bills. Investigative hearings, like the one into the events of January 6, 2021, gives Congress the right to subpoena witnesses to get to the truth.

The dramatic Watergate hearings in the Senate are legendary. Former White House counsel John Dean testified that President Nixon knew about the cover-up of the burglary at the DNC's headquarters, and Senator Howard Baker, a Tennessee Republican, asked the very important question about President Nixon: "What did the president know and when did he know it?" It was at the hearing that Nixon aide Alexander Butterfield mentioned that the president taped conversations in the Oval Office. It was the existence of those tapes that caused Nixon to resign.

IMPEACHMENT

The United States Constitution says that the House of Representatives "shall have the sole Power of Impeachment" (Article I, section 2) and "the Senate shall have the sole Power to try all Impeachments . . . [but] no person shall be convicted without the Concurrence of two-thirds of the Members present" (Article I, section 3). No one is above the law: the president, vice president, and all civil officers of the United States can be impeached for "Treason, Bribery, or other high Crimes and Misdemeanors." It is a key part of the "checks and balances" that the legislative branch has oversight of the executive branch.

The first step in an impeachment proceeding is for the House of Representatives to charge an official of the federal government by approving articles of impeachment. The articles of impeachment are then sent to the Senate, where they hold a trial. There are witnesses, and evidence is presented, and senators vote to either acquit or convict the impeached official. When it is a president who is on trial, it is the chief justice of the United States Supreme Court who is the presiding officer. In order to convict, the Constitution requires a two-thirds vote of the Senate (at least sixty-seven senators). If a conviction happens, the official is forced to leave office. Since 1789, about half of Senate impeachment trials have led to conviction and removal from office. No president has been removed from office by the Senate.

Former President Donald Trump is the first president to be impeached twice. He was impeached in the House in 2019 on charges of abuse of power and obstruction of Congress, but he was acquitted in the Senate. He was impeached the second time in 2021 by the House for inciting the insurrection that took place on January 6, when a violent mob broke into the Capitol as Congress was in session to certify the 2020 presidential election. Before Trump, only two other presidents had been impeached—Andrew Johnson in 1868 and Bill Clinton in 1998. Neither was convicted. Richard Nixon resigned in 1974 after articles of impeachment were drafted but before the House could vote on them. So far, every presidential impeachment case has fallen into what Congress considers to be "High Crimes and Misdemeanors."

It is generally agreed that "High Crimes and Misdemeanors" means a very significant abuse of office and of the public trust. The Senate has the power not only to vote to remove an official from office, but they can also hold a separate vote banning that person from ever holding office again. That did not happen to Trump.

★ ★ ★

Statuary Hall

One of the most symbolic and awe-inspiring rooms in the Capitol is Statuary Hall, a large theater-like room with statues positioned around its outer ring. Located just outside the House floor, members often walk through the space to vote. Since 1864, each state has donated statues of two citizens who they believe deserve to be honored, rotating out their choices occasionally. There are one hundred statues from the fifty states, and while at first they were all displayed in Statuary Hall, now only thirty-eight statues are there. In 1933, it was decided that it would be too crowded to have them all in one place. Today, statues are scattered throughout the Capitol complex.

Old House Chamber, designated as
National Statuary Hall by Lincoln in July 1864

The statues in this grand hall tell the stories of American icons—from presidents, like George Washington and Abraham Lincoln, to those who fought for recognition and justice, like Chief Standing Bear and Sojourner Truth. And we are reminded that these statues also tell the stories of real people who had lives and family members who loved them.

FAMILY VALUES

Lorna Rainey's great-grandfather Joseph Rainey was the first Black person to serve in the House of Representatives. In February 2022, when a room in the Capitol was dedicated to her great-grandfather, she was thinking not only about the fight he waged on behalf of justice for everyone, but also his private fight to make a better life for his own family. Joseph Rainey used his personal experience to make a powerful case for civil rights. The push for a new civil rights bill in 1873 had stalled in the Senate, and Rainey was worried that support in the House was waning. For most white members of Congress, the bill seemed much less urgent; they did not know what it was like to live in a country that didn't treat them as citizens. On a boat ride from Norfolk, Virginia, to Washington, D.C., Rainey was denied service in the main dining hall. In a pub in Washington, D.C., Rainey was charged much more for his glass of beer than the white customers. He had been taken by the collar of his shirt and kicked out of a whites-only restaurant. He had experienced racism firsthand. He asked his House colleagues: "Why cannot we stop at hotels here without meeting objection? Why cannot we go to restaurants without being insulted? We are here enacting laws of a country and casting votes upon important questions; we have been sent here by the suffrages of the people, and why cannot we enjoy the same benefits that are accorded to our white colleagues on this floor?"

It must have been emotional for Lorna Rainey to see her great-grandfather honored with his own room in the Capitol. He serves as an inspiration to so many people, but he is part of her family and a source of great pride to her personally. "He was a man of dignity, and he was going to prove a point that he was going to use whatever he could to draw attention to the fact that there was [a] lot of discrimination and racism in different types of establishments," she said. His legacy is a guiding light for her. "I always look at this and go, you know what? There's always going to be people who are going to try to stop you from doing what you want to do and fulfilling your potential and you just can't allow them to," Rainey said.

HONORING ALL AMERICANS

So much of the Capitol is about symbolism and grandeur, but it is important to remember that behind these marble and bronze statues, formal oil portraits, and room dedications, these are American lives and stories that touch so many people. Some of their experiences serve as painful reminders of the country's sins, including slavery and the way Native Americans were treated by early settlers, and that is why for too long they have been hidden from view.

As more and more people who were previously underrepresented get elected to Congress and a light is shone on their accomplishments, the rich and complicated history of the United States can be fully celebrated. An effort is finally being made to honor and showcase people from different backgrounds in rooms full of statues of mostly white men. In 2000, states were given the option to replace statues, and many leaders on the Confederate side of the Civil War have since been replaced. But there are at least eight statues of Confederates in the Capitol that no one can remove, not even members of Congress, without the approval of the state legislature and governor.

At the same time, there is a bronze bust of Martin Luther King Jr., one of the country's most celebrated civil rights leaders, in the Capitol Rotunda. It was unveiled on January

16, 1986, on the fifty-seventh anniversary of Dr. King's birth. And one hundred years after the birth of civil rights activist Rosa Parks, her statue was unveiled in Statuary Hall on February 27, 2013. It is the first full-length statue of a Black person in the Capitol. It is not part of the National Statuary Hall Collection, however, because it is not linked to any one state. The statue shows Parks, who is known as "the mother of the civil rights movement," seated and holding tight to her purse in a heavy coat as she waits to be arrested. During segregation there were certain places where Black people were allowed to sit. On December 1, 1955, Parks was commuting on a bus to her home from her job as a seamstress in a department store in Montgomery, Alabama. She sat in the front of the bus and refused to give up her seat to a white passenger. She was arrested and found guilty of disorderly conduct and being in violation of a local ordinance. Her courageous decision helped attract national attention, thus increasing pressure to pass the Voting Rights Act and desegregation.

Parks's niece, Urana McCauley, cried during the statue unveiling. She was forty-two, the same age her aunt was when she was arrested. "We talked about what it was like and how important it was for her to do what she did," she said, recalling their conversations. "It's so personal because I know what my aunt went through. And it was beyond just being physically tired. She was tired of the injustice."

Parks's act of civil disobedience was the result of years of frustration and anger at the oppression of Jim Crow segregation laws that mandated different schools, libraries, and bathrooms for Black people. She was active in the Montgomery chapter of the National Association for the Advancement of Colored People (NAACP), and on that day in 1955, her refusal to move to the back of the bus, where Black riders were supposed to sit, helped inspire a bus boycott led by Reverend Dr. Martin Luther King Jr. and other members of the civil rights movement. It lasted for more than a year. In 1956, the Supreme Court ruled that segregation on buses was unconstitutional.

"People always say that I didn't give up my seat because I was tired," wrote Parks in her autobiography, "but that isn't true. I was not tired physically. . . . No, the only tired I was, was tired of giving in."

In 1999, Rosa Parks was awarded the Congressional Gold Medal, Congress's highest honor. She passed away in 2005, and she was the first woman to lie in honor at the U.S. Capitol.

The Ponca Tribe had established their home in what is now northeast Nebraska long before Christopher Columbus's arrival in the Americas. Chief Standing Bear was born between 1829 and 1834 in the native lands of the Ponca Tribe in northern Nebraska. He became chief as a young man. When he was an adult, the land that had once been inhabited and maintained by the Ponca Tribe was stolen and developed by European settlers. Members of the Ponca Tribe were forced by the U.S. government to relocate to Oklahoma in 1877, but a year later, they were devastated by disease and starvation, with more than one-third of them dying. The government had promised farming equipment that never arrived, and by the time it did come, it was too late for planting. Chief Standing Bear lost his first son, Bear Shield, and his sister. His son had told him that he was worried that if he was not buried with his ancestors, he would be by himself in the afterlife. But in January 1879, when Standing Bear traveled to his son's birthplace in Nebraska to bury him, he was denied the right to bury his son where his son had requested. He was kept in custody in Fort Omaha. At that time, Native Americans could not leave their reservations, or area of land reserved for tribes, without the government's permission. The *Omaha Herald* ran an interview with Standing Bear, and his case was picked up by defense attorneys who challenged his detention. The government argued that Standing Bear could not sue because, as a Native American, he was not considered a "person" under the law.

During the trial on May 2, 1879, Chief Standing Bear made a powerful speech about his own humanity and the humanity of every Native American. He was the first Native American ever to testify in court. Through an interpreter, he delivered these history-making words: "My hand is not the color of yours, but if I pierce it, I shall feel pain. If you pierce your hand, you also feel pain. The blood that will flow from mine will be the same color as yours. The same God made us both. I am a man." On May 12, the judge issued his ruling that "an Indian is a 'person'" and has the rights enshrined in the Constitution. The judge's ruling was still racist; he called Native Americans a "weak, insignificant, unlettered and generally despised race."

Chief Standing Bear and those from his tribe who had

traveled with him were released from custody, and his son's remains were buried in his birthplace by the Niobrara River. Chief Standing Bear died there in 1908 and was buried beside his ancestors, just as his son had been.

In 1937, Nebraska chose to send statues of politician William Jennings Bryan and Julius Sterling Morton, who created a holiday for tree planting, to represent the state in Statuary Hall. Recently, lawmakers in Nebraska decided to replace both statues. Bryan was replaced by Chief Standing Bear, and Morton was replaced by a statue of iconic author Willa Cather, also from Nebraska.

Chief Standing Bear's dramatic statue is more than nine feet tall. His right arm is stretched out as he makes the case that the blood running through his hand is the same color as a white man's blood. The

A bronze statue of Chief Standing Bear, 2019, National Statuary Hall

black granite pedestal is low and wide, and on the steel frame there is a simple inscription:

NEBRASKA

CHIEF STANDING BEAR

Manchú-Nanzhín

c. 1829–1908

On the side of the pedestal, there are words from Standing Bear's moving statement he delivered in court. When his statue was dedicated in 2019, then Nebraska governor Pete Ricketts said he was honored to bring to light "one of the most important civil rights leaders in our country."

A bust of Sojourner Truth, a famous abolitionist and women's rights activist, was unveiled on April 28, 2009, in Emancipation Hall in the Capitol Visitor Center. It is the first sculpture in honor of a Black woman in the Capitol.

The event to dedicate the statue and celebrate Truth's life and tremendous accomplishments was led by three pioneering women: Nancy Pelosi, who became the first female Speaker in 2007; Hillary Rodham Clinton, who was the first woman to win the nomination of a major political party when she ran for president in 2016; and Michelle Obama, the first Black first lady.

"I hope that Sojourner Truth would be proud to see me, a descendant of slaves serving as the first lady of the United States of America," Obama said during the unveiling. "Now many young boys and girls like my own daughters will come to Emancipation Hall and see the face of a woman who looks like them."

Bust of Sojourner Truth, Emancipation Hall,
U.S. Capitol Visitor Center

Truth was born in 1797 in upstate New York, where her parents were enslaved. She was given the name Isabella Baumfree. She was first sold at auction at nine years old, and she had a series of enslavers before she escaped in 1826 with her baby daughter. When she learned that her son had been sold to an Alabama slaveholder, she dedicated her life to bringing him home. She said she summoned the strength of her faith in God and it made her "so tall within, as if the power of a nation was within [her]." She won her case to bring her son home, and in 1828, she moved to New York City, where she became an important figure in the women's rights and abolitionist movements. Her activism was tied deeply to her Christian beliefs.

She never learned to read or write, but she dictated her memoir, *The Narrative of Sojourner Truth*, and traveled the country speaking about slavery. In 1851, she spoke at the Ohio Women's Rights Convention in Akron and delivered her celebrated speech "Ain't I a Woman?" in which she called attention to the different experiences of being a Black and a white woman in America:

That man over there says that women need to be helped into carriages, and lifted over ditches, and to have the best place everywhere. Nobody ever helps me into carriages, or over mud-puddles, or gives me any best place! And ain't I a woman? Look at me! Look at my arm! I have ploughed and planted, and gathered into barns, and no man could head me! And ain't I a woman? I could work as much and eat as much as a man—when I could get it—and bear the lash as well! And ain't I a woman? I have borne five children, and seen most all sold off to slavery, and when I cried out

with my mother's grief, none but Jesus heard me! And
ain't I a woman? . . . If the first woman God ever made
was strong enough to turn the world upside down all
alone, these women together ought to be able to turn it
back, and get it right side up again!

Truth has remained a symbol of survival against all odds long after her death on November 26, 1883.

After a successful grassroots campaign, the state of Florida decided to replace the statue of Confederate general Edmund Kirby Smith, one of the last to surrender after the end of the Civil War in 1865, with a statue of educator and civil rights leader Dr. Mary McLeod Bethune. The eleven-foot-tall, 6,129-pound Italian Carrara marble is the first statue of a Black American, male or female, in the state collection in Statuary Hall. Her statue stands next to the sculpture of Rosa Parks.

Bethune was born in South Carolina in 1875 to parents who had been enslaved. She had a keen intellect, and because of her passion for education, she established an all-girls school for Black students with just $1.50 and only five students on the class roster. Several years later, the school merged with a boys' school and was renamed Bethune-Cookman College. It is now Bethune-Cookman University, a historically Black school that has thousands of graduates. Bethune was the first Black American woman to serve as a college president. Her statue was dedicated in July 2022. History was also made by the statue's sculptor, Nilda Comas, who is the first Hispanic artist of Puerto Rican descent commissioned to create a statue for the National Statuary Hall Collection. Comas's work shows Bethune wearing a long gown and a mortarboard cap with a tassel. Bethune devoted her life to educating Black people, and she herself had nine honorary doctorates. She was the founding president of the National Council of Negro Women, and she also served as vice president of the National Association for the Advancement of Colored People (NAACP).

Eleanor Roosevelt admired Bethune's trailblazing and tireless commitment, and in 1936, Franklin Delano Roosevelt named her director of the National Youth Administration's Division of Negro Affairs, which made her the highest-ranking Black woman in the U.S. government at the time. Bethune helped organize Roosevelt's unofficial "Black Cabinet" of advisers, the Federal Council of Negro Affairs. Her connection to the Roosevelts is depicted in the statue, which shows her hand resting atop a walking stick that had once belonged to President

Dr. Mary McLeod Bethune

Roosevelt. After his death, Eleanor gave it to her. In a 1949 radio broadcast about "interracial understanding," Eleanor said: "I, for one, am proud that our country could produce a Mrs. Bethune." Bethune passed away in 1955 when she was seventy-nine years old.

The inscription on the statue's pedestal, carved into the marble and highlighted in gold, reads:

FLORIDA
Dr. Mary McLeod Bethune
1875–1955

It is inscribed with one of Bethune's favorite quotes: "Invest in the human soul. Who knows, it might be a diamond in the rough."

Val Demings, who represented Florida as a Democratic congresswoman from 2017 to 2023, expressed what Bethune meant to her: "I remember as a little girl listening to my mother and father talk about a Black woman; a woman who looked like us, who started a college, here in Florida. As I listened to the story, it seemed impossible. Dr. Mary McLeod Bethune made what seemed impossible, possible."

It took nearly two decades for the statue of Harry Truman, the nation's thirty-third president, to be placed in the Rotunda. Truman is among a small number of presidents whose statues are in the Rotunda. He joins George Washington, Abraham Lincoln, James Garfield, Andrew Jackson, Ulysses S. Grant, Gerald Ford, Ronald Reagan, and Dwight Eisenhower. Alexander Hamilton's statue was moved from the Rotunda to the Hall of Columns to make space for Truman. Hamilton was the nation's first Treasury secretary, and he played an important role in ratifying the U.S. Constitution, but he was never elected president. Though he has become extraordinarily famous in recent years because of the Tony Award–winning Broadway show *Hamilton*.

Harry Truman represented Missouri in the Senate before he was named President Franklin D. Roosevelt's vice presidential running mate in 1944. Truman became president when, just eighty-two days into his term as vice president, he received a call on Capitol Hill and was told to report to the White House right away. FDR's wife, Eleanor Roosevelt, met Truman when he arrived and told him the stunning news that President Roosevelt had died. When Truman asked what he could do for her, Eleanor replied, "Is there anything we can do for you? You are the one in trouble now."

Truman came into office during an extraordinarily challenging time. World War II was ending in Europe but still raging in the Pacific, and a plan was needed to help rebuild parts of the world devastated by the war. Truman made the agonizing decision to drop atomic bombs on August 6 and 9, 1945, on two Japanese cities, Hiroshima and

Nagasaki, which killed hundreds of thousands of people. He worked to stop the spread of Communism, and he helped create the United Nations so that a war like World War II would never happen again.

Congressman Emanuel Cleaver of Missouri talked about another key accomplishment during Truman's presidency: his executive order desegregating military and government jobs. "With these necessary steps, President Truman helped create a Black middle class that enabled African Americans to advance in society and participate in the prosperity of this great nation," Cleaver said.

The bronze statue shows Truman mid stride. He loved walking, and after he left the presidency, he could often be found strolling from his home to his presidential library in Independence, Missouri. The front of the statue features his famous motto as president: "The Buck Stops Here," which acknowledges that as president, he was the one responsible for all decisions, both good and bad. At a reception after the unveiling of the statue of his grandfather, Clifton Truman Daniel was emotional. The world sees Truman as a president, while Daniel sees his grandfather.

He said that although it was a great honor, his grandfather was always a little bit embarrassed by statues. "I leave you today with my family's deep gratitude and a quote that illustrates those qualities in my grandfather," Daniel said. "'Do your duty and history will do you justice.'"

Harry S. Truman

Statues of two lesser known Arkansan figures from the eighteenth and nineteenth centuries are being replaced with these famous twentieth century Arkansas natives: singer Johnny Cash and civil rights activist Daisy Bates. Bates was the leader of the Arkansas NAACP and a mentor to the Black students who integrated Central High School in 1957, known as the Little Rock Nine. This latest swap is another example of how Congress is slowly becoming more representative by showcasing a broad range of people who have made a difference in their state.

★ ★ ★

The Cloakrooms
and the Hideaways

While the House, Senate, Rotunda, and Statuary Hall may be the well-known places within the Capitol—the places where visitors spend most of their time exploring—there are a number of rooms in the Capitol that few visitors ever get to see. In fact, there are some that even elected officials cannot see!

There is a House cloakroom off the floor of the House and a Senate cloakroom off the floor of the Senate. Both are places with seating areas, a snack bar, and even old-fashioned phone booths, where representatives and senators can relax or strategize. The phone booths are now used as private cubbies for cell phone conversations. There is a cloakroom for each political party and cloakroom attendants who work there. It is their job to tell lawmakers when a vote is coming. They also coordinate with pages to make sure that messages are delivered to the correct members of Congress.

Martin Paone worked in the Senate Democratic Cloakroom, and he was the Democratic Party secretary from 1979 until 2008. There is a Republican and a Democratic Party secretary who helps senators and their staff by advising them on the status of a bill, and they oversee the cloakroom. Because so few people get to actually step inside the cloakroom, Paone, who spent so much time there, provides a helpful description. He said the Senate Democrats' cloakroom is L-shaped, and the long part of the room has couches and tables so that members can sit and read and chat with each other. Paone described a desk at the end of the room where they can review their speeches before stepping onto the Senate floor to deliver them. They can bring staff in to rehearse arguments they'll make for or against a piece of legislation and to go over charts they plan to use to make their case.

It is a busy space with ten phone booths. Paone said these are "old wooden phone booths like Superman would change his outfit in, the old wooden phone booths that when you close the door the light goes on inside and there's even a little fan that goes on to circulate the air." Paone also recalled that "people call in, mostly from the offices, but once TV came in you'd get calls from all over the world. Mostly in the old days it was the offices and people downtown, wanting to know what's going on, especially in the days before they were on TV." Before email and cell phones, the landlines would be ringing off the hook. "Then you have five page lines, also, which were much busier in those days, prior to email. Email completely changed that. We used to run these kids ragged, running things around from office to office. That was the only way to get them. You know, whip notices would go out on Fridays to all senators' offices, and the kids would have to wait around for them to approve the whip notice so they could then bring them around to every Democratic office. All that changed with email." (More on pages and the page program later!)

In every cloakroom, there is a refrigerator, and the pages get to know the preferences of the senators so they can bring them water the way they like it to the floor before they begin

> **FUN FACT**
>
> In the late 1970s and early 1980s, Paone said there was a window that opened out to the hallway, and they used to open the window and joke with the tourists. "They'd be out there and you can hear them. The tour group would stop right outside the window, where there was a statue, and you could hear them talking and explaining it. Somebody in the cloakroom would occasionally open the window a crack and say [in an urgent voice], 'HELP ME, HELP ME.' You'd see these tourists look around, wanting to know where this was coming from."

speaking. Some prefer ice, some want it lukewarm, some prefer club soda. "In the olden days," Paone said, "we had Northern water and Southern water, as we called it. There was Poland Springs from Maine, and I can't remember the name, but the other water was from Arkansas. Eventually, we just stuck with Poland Springs." The pages began writing each senator's water preferences on paper and sticking it on the fridge.

Paone said Republicans allowed senators' staff to come into the cloakroom and stay even after the senator had left, whereas "other senators wanted the Democratic cloakroom to be more of a place that members could go and feel like that was a place that was their own, and talk among themselves without being encumbered by staff." It is easier when senators can talk and not feel like staff are eavesdropping and going to bring back a message to their bosses.

The cloakroom really functioned as an information hub, where members and staff could call in and receive updates about the status of votes. Before C-SPAN was televising what was happening on the floor of the House or Senate, the cloakroom was the only way to find out what was actually going on and when the next vote was going to take place, so that members of Congress could plan when they could leave for the day. Sometimes a member of a senator's staff might already have their coat on and be ready to walk out the door when a senator stands up and decides to give a forty-five-minute speech. It's just the way it goes.

Senators will have the cloakroom staff manage the list of people they need to talk to on a given day when they have time. A member of their staff will bring them letters to sign, and they will hand the letters to the cloakroom staff, who will assign a page to bring them back to their office. If they are working from the cloakroom all day, a page gets their lunch and they eat it in the cloakroom. It is always most crowded during a vote, and a line would form outside the phone booths back before cell phones. It was a place where they could build relationships. On Monday nights there would sometimes be a football game on the television. During baseball season, they'd have on games, and senators would be cheering for their favorite teams. Restaurant managers would call the cloakroom and ask, "Do we have to put out a buffet tonight?" or "Do we have to keep all these other people here to work the restaurant?"

The Senate defines a "vote-a-rama" as fifteen or more votes on a piece of legislation happening in one day. It can go on for hours because a senator can bring up an unlimited number of amendments, which all need to be voted on. On those days, the cloakroom is more than a hangout space; it is a bedroom too. Staff put out cots for senators to sleep in the cloakroom during vote-a-ramas.

SECRET OFFICES

There are some offices so secret that only a handful of people even know they exist. These are the senators' so-called hideaway offices near the Senate floor. There are no names on the doors to indicate whose is whose, but these offices are where senators go between votes for privacy and also for conversations they don't want anyone else to know about. Sometimes these offices are called Capitol offices so they sound more official and less top secret, but the fact remains that the location of most of these offices is strictly confidential.

These offices were created before senators had any designated offices to go to at all. The only place they were able to store their things was at their desks on the Senate floor. But once more space became available when the Supreme Court and the Library of Congress moved across the street, the senators who had served for the longest amount of time were given their own offices near the Senate floor, separate from the offices for their staff.

Leonard Ballard was the inspector of the Capitol Police from 1947 until 1984, and he called the senators' hideaway offices their own "little kingdom[s]." "You don't tell any person," Ballard said. "You know that a specific room is a senator's hideaway, because you see him going in there, but you don't tell anybody that, particularly the press." That sense of discretion, of knowing when not to talk, was what helped Ballard stay in the job as the most senior member of the police force for so long. "I think it is how I got along. I stayed here through . . . many changes of administration. . . . Nobody ever bothered with me."

The very best offices are reserved for members of Congress who have served the longest, regardless of which party they are members of. Some are small with no windows, but they give the senator a place to go to make a phone call or even to take a nap. At the start of each new session, senators get to choose a new hideaway office. Some of them may want to upgrade to a bigger office or a space with a nicer view, and others may want a change for different reasons altogether.

"In my old hideaway we had ghosts," said Vermont senator Patrick Leahy, who retired in 2023. "We had a three-hundred-pound table that we'd come in and find in different parts of the room that we hadn't left it in—it had moved around by itself about every two or three months."

★ ★ ★

The Speaker's Office

The presidency is mentioned more than eighty times in the Constitution and its amendments, but the Speaker's office appears just five times. Article I, Section 2, Clause 5 of the Constitution reads: "The House of Representatives shall choose their Speaker and other Officers; and shall have the sole Power of Impeachment." It is clear that the framers wanted the Speaker to be extremely powerful. They wanted the House to elect the Speaker, as opposed to the Senate, where the vice president presides. The Speaker is second in the presidential line of succession. Under the Twenty-Fifth Amendment, the vice president, the Speaker of the House, and the president pro tempore of the Senate are the first three people who would replace the president if he (or she) is no longer able to serve for any reason.

Members of the House vote for the Speaker publicly in a roll call vote (members say the last name of their choice out loud). They can vote for any candidate they prefer; however, they almost never vote for someone in the opposite party. In fact, the Speaker of the House does not even have to be a member of the House! Though they always have been.

The Speaker and their staff have offices in the Capitol in House office buildings alongside their colleagues. Across from the Speaker's Lobby is the room that now serves as the Speaker's Ceremonial Office, a space used to receive guests. It was once where the sergeant at arms worked. The room is decorated in Victorian style with a colorfully painted vaulted ceiling and floor tiles. For more than two centuries, the office has been home to an eleven-foot-tall walnut bureau with a flying eagle at the top and a bust of George Washington. The sculpture of Washington is one of the last remaining early busts in pristine condition.

The first person named Speaker of the House was Frederick Muhlenberg of Pennsylvania. Muhlenberg took office in 1789 when George Washington became president. Though the House has had a female speaker, the Senate still has not had a woman majority leader.

DID YOU KNOW?

Change happens slowly on the Hill, but when it does happen, it's at lightning-fast speed. On October 3, 2023, California Republican Kevin McCarthy became the first House speaker ever to be voted out of the job. But how did it happen? It was McCarthy who laid the groundwork for the vote to occur in the first place. In order to get the support of a key group of far-right Republicans, McCarthy agreed to a rule change that included "a motion to vacate." This meant that if just one Republican wanted to call for a no-confidence vote, they could do it and potentially end his speakership. And that's what happened! Florida congressman Matt Gaetz called for a no-confidence vote only nine months after McCarthy started the job. Gaetz represented a small group of Republicans who thought McCarthy was agreeing too much with the Democrats. The vote tally was slim, only 216 to 210, with eight Republicans agreeing with the Democrats to remove McCarthy from the speakership.

Afterward there was a period of several weeks of chaos while the post was vacant and Republicans were trying to find a replacement. The uncertainty during those weeks proves just how important the position is. Not only is the Speaker of the House second in the line of presidential succession, he or she speaks for the majority party in the House and helps craft and communicate legislative priorities. It is very difficult to hold on to power when the party is so divided.

★ ★ ★

The Vice President's Room

A lot of history has happened in the Vice President's Room, a room that few people even know exists. The vice president has an office in the West Wing, close to the Oval Office, as well as an ornate office in the Eisenhower Executive Office Building next to the White House. They also have an office in the Capitol, and because they must cast the tiebreaking vote in case of a stalemate, their office is just outside the Senate chamber for easy access. It was not until 1859 that the vice president was given the formal room in the Senate. The room, S-214, is elegantly decorated in late-nineteenth-century Victorian style. The desk in the Vice President's Room was actually used in the Oval Office by Presidents Nixon and Ford before it was returned to the Senate in 1977.

This office is used for press gatherings and ceremonies. But historic events have also happened in the vice president's Capitol Hill office. For example, President Ulysses S. Grant's vice president Henry Wilson died in the Vice President's Room in the Capitol after suffering a stroke in 1875. It is the room where Vice President Thomas Marshall signed the constitutional amendment that gave women the right to vote (though it only applied to wealthy white women at the time). When Vice President Harry Truman got the news that President Franklin Delano Roosevelt had died, he was in the Capitol. One of the last things he did was run to his office and grab his hat before going to the White House, where he was sworn in as president.

Vice presidents have only two constitutional duties: to succeed the president if he (or she) is unable to serve for any reason, and to act as president of the Senate to cast tiebreaking votes. The vice presidency is a difficult position because how much power and influence a vice president has depends entirely on the president and how much he (or she) will let them have. Benjamin Franklin suggested that the vice president be addressed as "Your Superfluous [meaning unnecessary] Excellency." Warren Harding's vice president, Calvin Coolidge, said: "I enjoyed my time as vice president. It never interfered with my mandatory eleven hours of sleep a day." Harry Truman, who served for less than three months as President Franklin D. Roosevelt's vice president, complained,

"The vice president simply presides over the Senate and sits around hoping for a funeral."

When the founding fathers gathered in Philadelphia in 1787 to write the Constitution, the office of the vice president was not something at the top of their minds. Article I, Section 3 of the Constitution states that the vice president will preside over the Senate "but shall have no vote, unless they be equally divided." Again, afraid of anything that could resemble a monarchy, the founders were concerned that a president may become too powerful if the vice president had any role in the Senate greater than serving as tiebreaker. And because of that concern, the vice president's job description was deliberately kept small. So, while a vice president can sit in the presiding officer's chair, he or she cannot even speak on the Senate floor without permission.

Vice President's Room, U.S. Capitol, circa 1923

A lot of power rests with the Senate. In fact, as we have learned, it is the job of the Senate to remove a sitting president from office. If a president is thought not to be well enough to do their job, then a two-thirds vote by Congress would allow their removal. That is, if a president objects, which

DID YOU KNOW?

Senate spouses have a bipartisan lunch on Tuesdays, and Roy Blunt, a Republican senator from Missouri from 2011 to 2023, said that his wife had to remind Karen Pence, the wife of then president Donald Trump's vice president, Mike Pence, that she was technically the president of the Senate Spouses Club. Lady Bird Johnson, Pat Nixon, Betty Ford, and Barbara Bush all took the position as the presiding officer of the Senate Wives Club (now the Senate Spouses Club in acknowledgment of the growing number of women in Congress) very seriously.

When George H. W. Bush became vice president in 1981, making Barbara Bush president of the Senate Spouses Club, she told the group: "I'm so happy to be here, I finally get to be a Senate wife!" (Bush ran unsuccessfully for the Senate twice, in 1964 and 1970.)

they probably would. If a vice president dies or is unable to serve, the president must name a successor to be confirmed by Congress.

Vice presidents have left their mark on the Capitol, where many of them once served as members of Congress. Marble busts of the vice presidents are placed throughout the Senate wing of the Capitol. "Being cast in marble is something every vice president looks forward to," joked Dick Cheney, who represented the state of Wyoming in the House from 1979 until 1989 before eventually becoming President George W. Bush's vice president years later. "It's not only a high honor, it's our one shot at being remembered."

★ ★ ★

PEOPLE

★ ★ ★

The Capitol Workers

The creation of the United States government by the founders of this country was a monumental achievement, as was the building of the Capitol, which has become the symbol of our democracy. And throughout the history of the Capitol, from the time it was built until today, there have been millions of people who have walked through these hallowed halls. History has been made almost on a daily basis, whether it is through a senator or representative arguing for a new law to be passed, groundbreaking testimony from American citizens on issues affecting their lives, debates being had over important concepts, or historical firsts that have been made. And it is only through these giant steps forward that our democracy can stay current, reflect the people of the United States, and flourish into the future. But in the midst of these historical firsts, there are also many, many people who work at the Capitol to keep it running. And without them, we wouldn't have the pristine grounds upon which our democracy sits and where conversations moving the country forward take place.

WORKING TO MAINTAIN THE PROPERTY

There are about eight hundred people who maintain the House side of the building, including people who work in carpentry, plumbing, heating and cooling, the Drapery Shop, the Carpentry Shop, the Upholstery Shop, and the Finishing Shop. It's a big family with people from all walks of life working in the same building. About the same number work on the Senate side, which John Bean, an electrician in the Capitol for more than forty years, said is like "college." The House side, which is much bigger and turns over more often, is like high school.

The workers who watch over and work hard to maintain the Capitol have different backgrounds, but they have one thing in common—their love of and dedication to preserving this important symbol of freedom.

WHO WORKS IN THE CAPITOL?

The building of the Capitol gave the newly formed government a place to come together, discuss, debate, and create the laws of the country. And over the decades, many senators, representatives, and other politicians have started their careers in the Capitol, learning the ways of government and trying to make a difference. (Of course, not everyone has come with such good intentions.)

Many presidents throughout history have served in Congress before entering the White House. Senators such as James Buchanan, James Monroe, Harry Truman, and others—seventeen in all—eventually became president. In the modern era, John F. Kennedy was a congressman and then a senator before becoming president, as was Barack Obama, who served in the Senate, and others as well. And Joe Biden, the forty-sixth president, spent thirty-six years in the Senate and served as chair of the Committee on the Judiciary and the Committee on Foreign Relations. He loved his years in the Senate and developed relationships in Washington, D.C., that helped propel him to the White House. He also appreciated the freedom he had as a senator. As vice president he answered to the president, as a senator he answered to his constituents, but, according to Biden, he was also his own boss. "In the good old days when I was a senator, I was my own man."

THE CAPITOL AS A REFLECTION OF THE COUNTRY

Visiting the Capitol can be an opportunity to think about our country, where it began, and where it is going. You almost feel gathered up in something bigger than yourself. But there are many people and groups who have been excluded throughout the almost 250 years of our country's existence. Congress has become more inclusive and now looks a little bit more like a reflection of America, but it still has a very long way to go. A century after the first woman was elected to Congress and a century and a half after the first Black congressman was seated, the Capitol has become a symbol of the path we've traveled and the strides we have made, but it is also a symbol of the long road still ahead.

In 2020, women made up 23.7 percent of the U.S. Congress, according to the Congressional Research Service. And 23 percent of voting members in the U.S. House of Representatives and Senate are ethnic or racial minorities. According to a Pew Research Center breakdown of data from the Congressional Research Service on the 117th Congress in 2021, 124 members of Congress identified as Black, Hispanic, Asian/Pacific Islander, or Native American. That is a 97 percent jump from the 107th Congress back in 2001–2003, when there were only sixty-three minority members.

The number of women and people of color in Congress is still not proportional to the percentage of women and people of color in the U.S. population. Seventy-seven percent of voting members of Congress are non-Hispanic white Americans, which is not in line with their 60 percent representation in the U.S. population. In 1981, 94 percent of

Congress members were white, and white people made up 80 percent of the population. This is all to say that they are still a much larger proportion of Congress than of the U.S. population.

The historian Henry Louis Gates Jr. points out that there was an almost ninety-year gap between the first two Black senators, Hiram R. Revels (1870–1871) and Blanche K. Bruce (1875–1881), and the third, Edward W. Brooke (1967–1979). In 1870, Hiram Rhodes Revels took his seat and became the first Black person to serve in Congress. At the time, he gave a passionate speech on the Senate floor and said, "I find that the prejudice in this country to color is very great, and I sometimes fear that it is on the increase." Bruce, who was born enslaved in 1841, was the first Black person to preside over the Senate (meaning he kept order in the Senate and recognized senators when they wanted to speak) in 1879. The racism he encountered in the Senate was sometimes on public display. Bruce represented Mississippi, and the other senator from the state, James Alcorn, refused to escort him to the front of the chamber when it was time to take the oath of office. New York senator Roscoe Conkling saw Bruce walking alone and went to his side. Before he became a senator, Brooke, who was the grandson of an enslaved person, was the first Black person to be elected attorney general of any state when he won the election in Massachusetts in 1962. He was reelected in a landslide in 1964. When he was elected to the Senate in 1966, he was the first Black person to win the popular vote. Bruce and Revels were elected by the Mississippi legislature and not by voters.

Senator Hiram Revels of Mississippi was the first African American member of the United States Senate. He took the oath of office on February 25, 1870.

Edward Brooke, United States Senator from Massachusetts, 1967–1979

Blanche Kelso Bruce

Victoria Claflin Woodhull

We might think that we live during the most divisive time in American history, but there has been a long history of members of Congress fighting with each other. Sometimes, the relationship between a senator and a member of the House of Representatives has gotten so bad that bills would not get passed simply because they refused to talk to each other. There have been times when the House and Senate would have to get an extension on certain bills because neither side would walk to the other side of the

Capitol to discuss the legislation. The issue was improved when the front of the Capitol was extended by thirty-two and a half feet and a conference room was created between the House and Senate side so that members would not have to concede and walk to the other side. It seems like members of either party still don't talk nearly enough.

The Fact-Checkers
(aka the Journalists)

The importance of getting at the absolute truth is clear, and journalists play a key role in that. From the House's first session in 1789, held in New York City's Federal Hall, journalists were there to inform the public about what the lawmakers they elected were up to. In 1802, the House voted to save space on the floor strictly for reporters.

Today in Washington, the credentialed members of the media, accredited by the Radio-TV Correspondents Gallery, work out of the House or the Senate press galleries. More than fifteen hundred correspondents with different media organizations, from daily print to online news to television, have permanent press credentials. Often the most candid conversations with members of Congress happen in the hallways when they are on their way to a vote or running to their offices. It is in those spontaneous moments that reporters are sometimes able to get their questions answered.

★ ★ ★

The Shops:

*The Finishing Shop, the Paint Shop,
and the Barbershop*

On a Thursday morning, Tim Magruder, who has worked on Capitol Hill for more than thirty-two years, starting in the cafeteria and now as the supervisor of the Finishing Shop, was sanding an enormous walnut wood frame. He held the sandpaper firmly in his right hand and went back and forth and back and forth. He was surrounded by pieces of furniture in various stages of refurbishment: wooden desks and the seal of the House of Representatives. He and his team in the Finishing Shop, located in the basement of the Capitol, were preparing for the transition when new members of Congress move in and retiring and defeated members leave. On the House side, this happens every two years; on the Senate side it takes place every six years. When

Tim Magruder working in the Finishing Shop

transitions happen, it's time for furniture pieces to get some TLC.

"Not many people make history for a job," Magruder said, taking a break from sanding. "That's what we do." He sees his work as a sort of art form. "Refinishing is my interpretation of what I want a piece of furniture to look like."

One of his favorite projects has been working on refinishing the House chamber dais and the benches that the members sit on.

On this day, the basement was buzzing with activity. Veteran Hershel W. "Woody" Williams was lying in honor as a symbol of the men and women who served in World War II. His catafalque, a platform that supports a coffin, had just been made and was in the Carpenter Shop. In the Paint Shop, painter Joe McGrane, who has worked there for five years, had cabinets on a table that he was painting a bright white color. There are samples of approved colors taped up on the wall—mostly Benjamin Moore paint is used. The white cinder block room is big, with jugs of paint lining the floors. There is a framed white sample on the wall with the note:

"Scuffy hallway walls." To McGrane, this feels like home, especially when an election is coming and there is so much work to do.

> ### DID YOU KNOW?
>
> Most of the workers at the Capitol either know someone or are related to someone who works there, or they help out with "the moves," the transitions after an election. The moves function as tryouts, when workers are hired temporarily during busy times to show off their skills. If they are good enough, they get hired full-time.

THE BARBERSHOP

Giuseppe "Joe" Quattrone spent more than five decades giving Republicans and Democrats haircuts in the small barbershop in the basement of the Rayburn House Office Building. He was an institution for lawmakers and their staffers alike, and was known as Joe Q.

The walls of the barbershop are lined with autographed images of Joe Q and all the politicians he has known since the 1970s. After nearly fifty-two years, he retired in the summer of 2022, at eighty-eight years old. When he was working, he wore a robin's-egg blue smock, and his hair was held back in a white ponytail. A well-worn comb, missing some of its teeth, was usually in his breast pocket. The shop's wood paneling and leather chairs harken back to an earlier time.

He gave "a great haircut, but it's more than a haircut," said Howard A. Denis, senior counsel for the House Committee on Oversight and Accountability.

Quattrone was friends with many of the people whose hair he cut, and spent uninterrupted time with each of them as he worked his magic. "This is a family barbershop," Quattrone said. "We got a lot of friends who come in, shoot the breeze."

Quattrone started cutting hair in Italy when he was just twelve years old. In 1952, he left Italy for Ohio, where he lived with his brother and uncle, and later moved to Washington. He called his congressman, and that is how he got the job. By the 1980s, he was in charge of the barbershop, which was privatized, which means it was transferred from public to private ownership, in the mid-1990s. The shop still offers incredibly inexpensive haircuts. Anyone can get their hair cut there, but it is a well-kept secret. There are four barbers— three men and one woman—and Joe Q was its life-force.

"I came here like a fish out of water, and look where I'm at, the best job in the world," he said in an interview with a Washington news station shortly before he retired. "It's the best job because you come in contact with everybody." He enjoyed learning from everyone, from the janitors who work at the Capitol to the president of the United States!

Back when Quattrone began cutting hair on the Hill in the early 1970s, there were five barbershops on the House side with fourteen barbers, four shoe shiners, and three manicurists. Now there's just one.

"I think it's one of the best jobs a barber can have," Quattrone said. "I got the most famous people, the most important people. And I'm a part of it."

House barbershop menu

It is the same for Senate barber Mario D'Angelo, who has been working in the Capitol for more than forty-five years. He works in a shop in the basement of the Russell Senate Office Building, which is just a bit more modern but still very much tied to the past. Haircuts are inexpensive there too; in fact, they were free until 1979! That's when senators were tired of criticism over their free haircuts, so the barbershop started charging $3.50, which was much less than the going rate of $15.

In recent years, even the barbershop has been affected by growing partisanship in the country. "Every step of the way things have changed on the Hill," D'Angelo said. Things have gotten hard. "It has separated people. People don't speak to each other as much as they used to."

But within the walls of the barbershop people can finally relax. The allegiance members of the House of Representatives feel toward the House barbershop is shared by senators for the Senate barbers. In 2019, then Senate minority leader Chuck Schumer, a Democrat from New York, took a moment on the Senate floor to acknowledge the death of someone who was part of what he called "the Senate family." "David Miles Knight—the beloved barber in our barbershop—one of the Senate's master barbers for the last thirty-six years, lost a lengthy battle with cancer," said Schumer. "He was always eager to ask about a customer's day or a colleague's weekend, and just as eager to regale those folks with stories about his family."

According to a 2010 report on the history of the Senate barbershop published by the Senate sergeant at arms, the barbershop goes back to the nineteenth century. In its earliest days, the shop was in the Capitol and was built alongside bathrooms "to help senators cope with the dirt and distances of Washington" well before there were paved roads. "Arguing that the irregular schedules of Senate clientele would hamper a private business, the Senate funded the barbershop's utilities and products and paid the salaries of barbers," the report explains. For years, every single senator (they were all male up until 1932, when Hattie Caraway became the first woman elected to serve a full term—she had entered the Senate in 1931 to replace her husband, who had died in office, and then she won election on her own) received a gold-trimmed shaving mug inscribed with his name. Presidents Andrew Johnson and Teddy Roosevelt visited the shop as well.

As it is for people working in the White House, being able to keep secrets is very important. Barbers rarely share any private moments that happen inside the shop. "I heard a lot of conversations between senators," Senate barber Elbert Link said in 1981, "but I never talked about it with anyone."

★ ★ ★

The Restaurant and Dining Staff

In 1858, House Speaker James Orr instituted the House Members' Dining Room in the Capitol, where "wholesome refreshments" would be available. In its early years, George Downing, a restauranteur and civil rights activist, ran the Members' Dining Room from 1868 to 1876. He turned it into one of the most popular restaurants in Washington! He was such an important part of it that it became known as Downing's Restaurant. Downing fought for school desegregation, was active in the Underground Railroad, and used his relationships with members of Congress to make his case for civil rights.

Decades later, in the 1950s, the House Members' Dining Room had an old-school list of offerings, and back then, everything was under one dollar. There were skinless frankfurters and stewed potatoes and something called "half-and-half and graham crackers," which sounds like a very strange dessert. Over the years, people's tastes have changed, and the offerings have been replaced with more traditional soups, salads, and sandwiches. And while there are more appealing dishes, the bean soup has been the mainstay on the menu. In 1904, Speaker Joe Cannon directed that bean soup "be served in the House every day, regardless of the weather."

Fred Johnson once ran the meal service on board Air Force One, the president's plane, and he left to oversee thirteen dining outlets spread across five buildings in the Capitol complex. One of his favorite parts of the job is creating a four-hundred-pound, seven-foot-wide gingerbread replica of the Capitol to display every Christmas. He is a U.S. Air Force veteran of twenty years who went through culinary training. "We aren't political people," Johnson said of his staff. "When the House flips, we're still going to be here making the quality of life as good as it can be for members."

Most of the time, he loves his job because meals bring people together. "When you're walking around Capitol Hill with a chef coat you meet a lot of people!" he said.

One of Johnson's good friends, John Bean, was an electrician in the Capitol for over forty years. He started working at the Capitol when he was sixteen years old, cutting the grass as a groundskeeper. Johnson and Bean used to meet for lunch at Longworth cafeteria almost every day. A librarian from the Library of Congress would join them, along with a staffer from the parking garage, a House photographer, and someone from the badge office who issued IDs. They had a regular table, ordered the same thing, and helped each other out. Johnson knew people in all the shops. "If I needed a table saw or a vacuum cleaner, I knew who to ask," Johnson said. He needed the table legs trimmed off a stainless steel table and went to friends who worked in the metal shop. "I gave them a couple dozen doughnuts as a thank-you."

Even though meals in the Capitol are more informal now, there are reminders everywhere of how special the place is. Above the entrance to the House restaurant, there is a message that serves as a reminder to members who take the time to look up:

Man is not made for the state
but the state for man
and it derives its just powers
only from the consent of the governed.

Robert Remsburg was the head chef at the House Members' Dining Room from 1995 to 1997. When Congress was in session, he would serve three hundred members lunch over the course of two hours. He worked in a small kitchen and was shoulder to shoulder with his cooks. The main kitchen was downstairs and had to have a two-person elevator to bring up food. There was a sense of community that he treasured.

The staff tried to keep the conversation away from controversial subjects, even though decisions were being made by the people they served that directly affected their lives. "It's like any job," Remsburg said, "you don't talk politics or religion."

Tina Panetta also worked as a restaurant staffer. She was born on November 13, 1925, in the small town of Ovindoli, Italy, a German stronghold during World War II. She lived through the war and moved to the United States in 1955 to make a better life for herself. In 1960, her eldest brother, Antonio, became the head chef of the Senate Dining Room and his best friend, Pasquale, became the head chef in the House Members' Dining Room.

One day when she was visiting Antonio, Tina was asked if she wanted a job as a waitress. She still could not speak English, but she learned. She started her twenty-three-year career on January 19, 1968, working in the Senate dining room.

Almost fifty years later, in 2016, Tina Panetta's grandson Gian lived with her in Silver Spring, Maryland, when he

Tina Panetta in the Senate Dining Room

interned on the Hill. He heard story after story about her from the senators she'd served, even though she had been retired for twenty-six years by then. "She brought that motherly vibe to the Capitol," he said. When she turned ninety-five, he asked senators to call her and write her an email. Many of them did!

"She's a simple person in a complex world . . . she wants to know how her grandkids are doing, what's currently going on is not a big part of her life. What made her so attractive to senators was asking them, 'How are the kids?'" Senators would bring her gifts back from trips, Gian said. She was never intimidated by the senators, and everyone wanted her to be their waitress.

Because many senators have gone on to be president, Tina forged relationships with them before they got to the White House. Once she was serving then senator Joe Biden as he sat alone at his table. Biden was a Delaware senator for almost four decades before he was vice president and then president. As Tina finished pouring his coffee, Dr. Jill Biden and their young sons, Hunter and Beau, walked into the dining room. The boys immediately rushed to their father's table with smiles on their faces, giving him a big hug as he lifted them both up in his arms. Tina reminisced about how "cute" Hunter and Beau looked in their "little suits." Tina held back her tears of happiness as she served them. The boys had survived a terrible car accident that killed Biden's daughter, their sister Naomi, and first wife, their mother Neilia.

More recently, Maryland congressman Jamie Raskin talked about Panetta on the House floor and used her nickname, Mother on the Hill. "At a time of polarization," Raskin said, "Tina's story reminds us of our common bonds both in Congress and in the country."

★ ★ ★

The Cobblers of the Capitol

Emmanuel Bolden, thirty-one, has been working beside his father, Alvin, who is seventy-five years old, since 2016. Alvin, whom Emmanuel lovingly calls Pops, taught Emmanuel how to do his job. The Boldens are cobblers who take care of lawmakers' shoes. Alvin worked as a cobbler in the House barbershop for years and now works next to his son in the subway entrance in the Rayburn House Office Building. Amid the whirring of the subway car whisking members to and from their offices or to the floor for debates and votes, the Boldens enjoy their time together.

"It's been a magical journey," Emmanuel said, sitting on a stool in front of two black leather tufted seats during a lull in his workday. "I learned to do the job with patience and respect. You have to love what you do. If you love what you do, the money and reward come naturally."

He has many longtime customers who have become friends. Alvin taught Emmanuel what he considers to be an important rule: never discuss politics or religion. And keep your personal business to yourself. But if you have to talk, Alvin said, be sure to ask questions. He told his son, "I always met people who knew more than I did."

Alvin also taught his son to take his time, but Emmanuel said he often has to do a job that should take thirty minutes in fifteen minutes. His clients are mostly members of Congress and their aides, who are always in a rush. "He taught me the trade and technique; you have to be slow and steady because the more patience you have the better it turns out. It needs tender loving care like anything else. My dad always wanted better for me. He lets me know that your work is a reflection of what you do, whether it's shining shoes or anything else."

Alvin Bolden was born in 1947 and started working at the Capitol in 2008 as a shoe shiner. But he had lots of experience in the business. He started working as a shoe shiner when he was just twelve years old at a barbershop in Washington, D.C. That is where he learned the art of shining shoes so they look brand-new. He worked in the House barbershop for several years side by side with his good friend Joe Quattrone.

"I did the feet, and he did the hair," Alvin said with a

laugh. "Our customers were pretty much the same. It was killing two birds with one stone."

The Boldens want their shared shoe-shining station to be "an oasis" for members. "The shoe shop is a place for them to unwind. The last thing they want to do when they walk into our shop is talk shop. This is a place where they can turn off politics and just be themselves. That's the experience I want. The shoe shining is just the cherry on top," Emmanuel said with a broad smile.

★ ★ ★

The Subway Car Operators

Very few people know that there's an entire subway located below the Capitol for members of Congress as well as visitors. But underground congressional travel began more than a hundred years ago, in 1909. The subway was initially designed to connect the Capitol to the Russell Senate Office Building. It brings members safely and quickly from their office to their chambers in the Capitol when they need to vote, sometimes several times a day.

The subway was originally two roadways with two old-fashioned Studebaker cars, affectionately called Tommy and Peg. Each car could hold ten passengers. There were no train tracks, so it was quite dangerous. Cars had to back up to turn around, and there was a real concern that a senator could be run over. In 1912, the cars were replaced with monorail

Monorail subway from Capitol to Senate

vehicles that went back and forth on electric tracks. They had uncomfortable wicker benches facing each other, so there was not a moment of privacy. In 1960, a driverless monorail was put in place for the Dirksen Senate Office Building, and in 1982, the line was extended to reach the Hart Senate Office Building. It was replaced by an automatic train in 1992.

The Senate subway is where reporters gather to question lawmakers as they head to and from the Capitol and their office buildings. The train goes slow and steady over its quarter-of-a-mile run. It goes just fifteen miles an hour during the forty-four-second ride (the walk takes about a minute and twenty seconds). But the ride can be a place where alliances are made and broken.

Daryl Chappelle was the U.S. Senate underground subway operator for forty-four years. When nervous young staffers new to the job asked Chapelle for directions, he tried to calm their nerves and reassure them that everything would be all right. He kept a smile on his face when impatient senators used a buzzer to signal they were in a hurry. Chappelle retired in 2014, outlasting most members of Congress! When he retired, he had made an estimated 130,000 trips escorting senators from the Capitol to their office buildings. From his post on a swivel seat inside the small open-air train, he witnessed some of the most impactful moments in history, including the Watergate scandal and senators considering whether to impeach President Nixon for his role in it, and September 11.

Although Chappelle saw so many historical moments, he never set foot on the Senate floor until he retired. Senators and staffers stood in line to shake Chapelle's hand, and reporters signed goodbye cards for him. A group of Senate leaders praised his work as they got up on the Senate floor one by one and thanked him.

"He has a smile [that] covers his whole face," said Democrat Harry Reid when Chapelle retired.

"He's the happiest guy you ever met," declared Republican Mitch McConnell. "He has a genius for lifting people's spirits."

Meanwhile, in the House of Representatives, members had to walk between their offices and the Capitol until the Rayburn House Office Building opened in 1965. All those years before, they watched jealously as senators took air-conditioned rides on their own train system while they had to endure the excruciating summer heat. House members walked—and sometimes even had to run—when the legislative signal bells rang and they had to vote in the Capitol. But the House Office Building Commission considered a train unnecessary.

Finally, the Rayburn House Office Building was finished, complete with its own parking garage, gym, and a two-track

Andre Washington at the controls of the subway that travels between the U.S. Capitol and the Russell Senate Office Building

subway to and from the Capitol. It was on January 15, 1965, that a crane lifted the gray train car from a flatbed truck and into the tunnel. Inside the thirty-foot train sat Maryland representative Clarence Long. He wanted to be the first person to ride the subway, except he did not do it horizontally; he did it vertically! Long said it was "probably the most unusual subway car ride" he'd ever taken. After its installation, the *Baltimore Sun* newspaper published a story calling attention to the subway's "elegant" twenty-four seats and high windows, designed to keep the congresspeople's hair in place during the ride.

Today, Dave Anderson operates the subway car from the Rayburn House Office Building to the Capitol, ferrying members of Congress to and from their offices in order for them to vote. He also meets curious visitors who have come to see members of Congress representing their state or just to get a peek at the majestic Capitol dome.

Anderson is in the military and is licensed to drive tractor trailers, bulldozers, and even tanks. He started working at the Capitol in 2011 and, like so many people who work there, he has family on the Hill—his brother-in-law works across the Capitol complex at the Senate subway station. He maintains the train and works on elevators and escalators. Anderson said he likes maintenance and problem-solving, and he likes asking members of Congress why they decided to run for office. He says that some of the interns who ride the train tell him that they'll be back, but when they return they will be members of Congress themselves.

"We'll be sitting in that seat one day," they say, pointing to the Members Only seat reserved for congresspeople.

"I'll be looking out for you!" Anderson tells them.

The subway is still popular because it makes life easier. Now members of Congress rely on the Capitol Subway System in the fluorescent-lit basement every day Congress is in session. It is especially helpful during the warmer months, when Washington heat can be brutal, and in the winter when it's cold. But the train operators love this system as well.

"The people you meet on the train make or break it for you," Anderson said. "The job can get boring, but they keep you sane because you meet new people all the time."

★ ★ ★

The Doorkeepers

The House and Senate each have a sergeant at arms (SAA) who works with the U.S. Capitol Police to protect lawmakers, their staff, and visitors. In the Senate, the Office of the Sergeant at Arms and Doorkeeper was created to keep senators in Washington and focused on business. The Senate Sergeant at Arms and Doorkeeper controls who has access to the Senate floor, and they also keep order on the floor. They are also charged with keeping senators safe when they're in the Capitol complex. It is a powerful and very important gatekeeping and law-keeping position.

But the term "doorkeeper" doesn't really tell us everything that the job entails. When the president or a foreign leader visits the Senate, the doorkeeper escorts them onto the Senate floor. And when a senator dies in office, it is the doorkeeper who plans the funeral. They also work on inauguration plans for the swearing-in ceremonies of newly elected senators. The sergeant at arms leads the senators from the Senate to the House Chamber for joint sessions of Congress and to the inaugural platform for the president's swearing-in. As the chief law enforcement officer of the Senate, the sergeant at arms also keeps the Capitol and all Senate buildings—including the Senate floor, chamber, and galleries—safe. Because of the immense responsibility, the Office of the Sergeant at Arms and Doorkeeper has the biggest staff and largest budget in the entire Senate. In addition to safety, the SAA is charged with all computer and telecommunications services. The SAA also shares responsibility for the U.S. Capitol Police and the Senate Page Program, among other departments. So if being a doorkeeper sounds like a straightforward job, at the Capitol it is anything but!

In the House of Representatives, the doorkeeper served from 1789 until 1995, when the position was dissolved. As on the Senate side, the doorkeeper controlled access to the House Chamber and eventually oversaw the press in the gallery. Over the years, thirty-four people were House doorkeepers, until the position ended when Republicans took control of Congress and eliminated the position in an effort to save money. Many of the doorkeeper's duties were transferred to the sergeant at arms, the clerk of the House, and the newly

Doorkeepers, House of Representatives, 1920

created chief administrative officer.

The last House doorkeeper was James T. Molloy, who started in the position in 1973 and left in 1995. Most Americans saw the House doorkeeper when he introduced presidents before the State of the Union and addresses before the joint sessions of Congress. But there is a lot of work that goes on behind the scenes. As doorkeeper, Molloy controlled a multimillion-dollar budget and oversaw hundreds of jobs, including pages. He also managed the House barbershop and the press galleries, among other areas of the sprawling institution. He put together more than seventy joint sessions of Congress, including deciding on the seating chart. It was up to him to determine which congressional spouses would get the best seats!

William "Fishbait" Miller was the congressional doorkeeper

before Molloy, serving from 1949 until 1953 and again from 1955 to 1973. The reason for the short gap in his service was because from 1953 until 1955, the House was controlled by the Republican Party, and Miller served as minority door-keeper because Democrats were in the minority. Miller was from a small town in Mississippi near the Gulf Coast. He first arrived in Washington in 1933 and took a job as a clerk in the House post office. Then he was messenger to the door-keeper, a job also held by Lyndon Baines Johnson, who went on to become the thirty-sixth president of the United States.

"As messenger to the Doorkeeper," Miller wrote in his memoir, "I got to see everything that was going on in and out of the House chambers. I started to learn how bills were passed. It is a long and cumbersome ordeal, and for every bill that is passed perhaps five hundred fall by the wayside."

Miller was chatty and likable, and he became famous for his booming voice when he announced the arrival of the presidents to speak before a joint session of Congress or when they gave the State of the Union. It was the doorkeeper's job to make sure that members of the Supreme Court and other officials would come to the Hill for the address delivered by "the Old Man." (Miller wrote that "the President is always called 'the Old Man' by those who protect him, whether he is as old as Eisenhower or as young as Kennedy." Hopefully, when we have a female president, they will have to change that wording!)

Miller would announce the president's arrival with a thunderous declaration—"Mistuh Speakah—the Prez-dent of the Yoo-nited States"—that reverberated through the halls of Congress for nearly twenty-five years. He introduced six presidents at joint sessions of Congress as well as other visitors. He oversaw 357 employees, including pages, janitors, and barbers, as well as an annual budget of $3.5 million.

Most of the people who worked in the Capitol loved Miller, who lived by the motto: "Everyone's important here." The Capitol was like his second home; sometimes he wandered around the halls in bare feet while his shoes were in the House barbershop being shined.

Decades have passed since Miller left, but Sergeant William McFarland was sworn in as sergeant at arms in 2023 and will be expected to perform many of the same duties. He is the thirty-ninth person to hold this position since the first sergeant at arms took care of security when Congress met in New York City. McFarland began working on Capitol Hill in 1991 when he was a security aide for the Capitol Police.

FUN FACT

The State of the Union is a tradition that was started when George Washington delivered his annual message to Congress. Since 1947, it has generally been known as the State of the Union address, named when President Harry Truman gave the first televised address.

WHAT HAPPENS AT THE PRESIDENT'S STATE OF THE UNION ADDRESS?

That booming voice announcing the president of the United States comes from the House sergeant at arms. It is the sergeant at arms who escorts the president into the House Chamber before the president delivers the State of the Union address as millions of people watch from home on television. It is the sergeant at arms who dramatically announces, "Mr. Speaker, the president of the United States." The person who announces the president practices over and over again beforehand to make sure their voice can be heard well throughout the large and crowded House Chamber.

The State of the Union address is a giant production to say the least. There are four doctors, five nurses, and five corpsmen who are stationed around the chamber. Two additional doctors are close by, standing near the president's White House doctor. This is because the most important people in government are gathered together in one place.

The doorkeeper announces members of the Supreme Court, who then walk into the chamber. Then the sergeant at arms announces members of the president's cabinet: "Mr. Speaker, the members of the president's cabinet." Everyone rises and applauds, and then the cabinet members seat themselves according to the date on which each was made a member of the executive branch.

Once everyone is seated, the electrician turns on the floodlights and the microphones. The show begins! There is always an excitement that one can feel in the chamber before the president enters. It can be very overwhelming, and some presidents were too nervous to enjoy the moment. President Harry Truman always asked for two glasses of water and would take sips throughout the evening to calm his nerves. President Dwight D. Eisenhower was the first president to wear pancake makeup when he addressed Congress, always aware of the fact that it was televised. Eisenhower was especially worried that the bright lights would make the top of his bald head shine, so extra makeup was applied there.

After the State of the Union, the opposing political party offers a live televised rebuttal, or a response to the priorities laid out by the president. Since 2004, there has also been a Spanish response to the president's annual address or State of the Union speech, intended to reach a growing part

FUN FACT

A State of the Union address must happen one year after the president is elected so that he (or she) can speak to the country's challenges.

of the electorate. Then governor Bill Richardson of New Mexico delivered the first Spanish language response, in which he was critical of George W. Bush's immigration policies and the effect his presidency had on the Hispanic community. In rare instances, the English and Spanish responses are delivered by the same person. For example, in 2013, Republican senator Marco Rubio was the first official to do both, taping his Spanish-language version first and delivering his English response live on television.

FUN FACT

One member of the president's cabinet is purposely not on the guest list to watch the State of the Union address. This is done in case something devastating happens, like a natural disaster or a terrorist attack, and someone needs to assume the presidency. The tradition started during the Cold War, when there was fear that a nuclear attack from the Soviet Union could destroy Washington, D.C. After the September 11 attacks, that fear grew stronger. The so-called designated survivor is usually a Cabinet member far down the line in presidential succession. They watch the State of the Union on television from a secure location so that, should anything happen, they are far away from harm.

DID YOU KNOW?

When foreign heads of state visit Washington, it is the doorkeeper's job to make them feel welcome on Capitol Hill. Tradition holds that the head of state would attend a formal dinner at the White House, known as a state dinner. The morning of the second day, the secretary of state and a protocol officer would visit them at Blair House—across Pennsylvania Avenue from the White House—also known as the president's guesthouse. From there, the doorkeeper, now the sergeant at arms, escorts them to the Capitol, where they address a joint session of Congress. If the president is not there, it is referred to as a joint meeting. If the president is there—which is rare—then it is referred to as a joint session of Congress. After the speech, the foreign dignitary is escorted to lunch on the Senate side of the Capitol and treated as a guest of honor. The ambassador to the United States from the visitor's country is there and so is the secretary of state, the hosts of the Senate Committee on Foreign Relations and the highest-ranking members of the House Foreign Affairs Committee.

A ROYAL VISIT AND A ROYAL GAFFE!

In 1951, Queen Elizabeth II, who was then the crown princess of England, and her husband, Prince Philip, came to Washington for a visit that did not include a speech at Congress. But they went to the Capitol, and President Harry Truman told William Miller to show her around. Truman had warned the prince and princess at dinner the night before that they would be meeting Miller, who was "a real character." Even though Congress was not in session, several members stayed to meet the royals.

Miller greeted the princess on the Capitol steps with a handshake and a lighthearted "howdy, ma'am" before taking her arm and leading her to the House Chamber. No one talks to royalty that way, so she was caught off guard.

"Wave to the boys and girls in the gallery," Miller instructed the princess. "She looked at me a little strangely, but she did so with a very refined little hand wave." When he interrupted Prince Philip, who was being escorted by someone else, and asked him to do the same, Miller recalled in his memoir, Prince Philip "looked a little startled." After they left Washington, Truman told Miller: "Well, Fishbait, I warned them, and you sure didn't let me down."

Because of his famous royal flub, Miller was made to attend protocol school at the State Department if he wanted to keep his job. The protocol office might not have been completely satisfied though, because they had to start giving him note cards with instructions when a foreign head of state came to town.

* * *

The Pages:

An Entryway into Politics

There is a program in Washington, D.C., for people who are too young to run for office but who want a hands-on experience working on the Hill. The program was designed for young people to serve as messengers in the Capitol. The U.S. Senate sergeant at arms hires pages, who then "play an important role in the daily operation of the Senate." Pages prepare the chamber for Senate sessions, work on the Senate floor to assist during roll call votes, and they support senators and staff during debates. Pages have all sorts of interesting jobs on the Hill, and the program offers an incredible close-up look at how democracy works.

The experience pages have also shines a light on different eras in American history and lets us look at history from the perspective of a young person. Hundreds of years ago, pages

154

were very young. During the Civil War, Albert Pillsbury became a page when he was just eleven years old! He traveled from Chelsea, Massachusetts, to Washington, D.C., where he lived at several boardinghouses from 1862 to 1867. Pillsbury told his mother what was happening during his exciting years in Congress. One of his most interesting letters was when the House passed the Thirteenth Amendment, abolishing slavery on January 31, 1865. "When the Speaker announced that [the amendment] had passed, everybody in the galleries cheered, waved their handkerchiefs, the members hurrahed, threw up their hats, threw up books, papers, anything they could lay their hands upon . . . I never saw such thundering applause. . . ."

Representative Thomas Hubbard of New York wrote a letter to his wife describing what pages did in those early days. "We have a charming little boy about 12 years old who waits on the House," Hubbard wrote, "and when a member rises to submit a resolution the little fellow leaps around lightly and with the swiftness of an arrow stands by his side. . . ." The boy, named Oswald, stood by any member who was going to speak before the House and "if anything is submitted in writing, he takes it and conveys it to the clerk who sits under the Speaker's chair, then takes his leave and watches till another member rises when the same ceremony takes place again."

Oswald and the other early pages, some of whom were

as young as eight years old, also gave members glasses of water when they were delivering long speeches. Much of the work of the page was very physical. Capitol Hill pages would deliver messages for members from different offices to the floor, and they would raise the U.S. flag over the House when the House was in session. They also filled inkwells, lit lamps, and wandered the halls to announce when there were votes. Sometimes, when a vote was held late at night, they would travel to the members' Washington homes and wake them up so they could come back and vote. Some pages were referred to as "riding pages" because they went on horseback or in horse-drawn buggies to deliver messages from members to federal government agencies around the city. The most revered page was the Speaker's page, who would escort the Speaker to the House floor and who had an especially important job because they worked for the most powerful member of Congress.

By 1838, there were eighteen young boys working as messengers in the House of Representatives. Most were chosen because they were the children of influential people and members of the House and the Senate. Sometimes, though, they were local boys without families in Washington, D.C., who needed the small salary the program provided to get by. They were paid $1.50 a day ($40 today), and from time to time, members gave them as much as $250 (more than $6,500 today!) at the end of each congressional session. By the early

Representative Longworth and House pages, 1925

twenty-first century, pages made more than $20,000 a year. Before the practice was banned, pages could make money on the side selling books to tourists with members' signatures, and they even sometimes sold copies of members' speeches.

Pages usually served between one and four years, so they needed to balance school and work. But it was only in 1926 that the House started sending pages to school. At first, they were educated by a tutor in the basement of the Capitol, but then the Capitol Page School was established for House and Senate pages in 1931. They went to school in the early morning, broke for work in the Capitol, and returned to school in the late afternoon, when floor business was done for the day. By the 1950s, the school was located on the third floor of the Jefferson Building of the Library of Congress. It was a lot like other public high schools, except its students had very interesting after-school jobs. And they had an incredible view of the National Mall. One student called it "clearly the most magnificent high school campus in the world." For decades, the pages lived in boardinghouses around the Capitol before a dormitory was set up for them in the 1980s.

In the twentieth century, the program accepted pages from all over the United States, and instead of being based on who the children were related to or whether they needed the money, it was based on their academic performance. The House program ended in 2011 because it was too expensive to maintain and because technology had made much of the job unnecessary. Now that every member and their staff has cell phones and access to emails, they don't need anyone to deliver messages on their behalf. However, the Senate page program has continued, in part because the Senate has always valued tradition so highly. To this day, in the Senate, pages deliver messages and legislative information to members of

Congress, and they carry bills and important amendments to the presiding officer's desk. The pages in the Senate must be at least sixteen years old, and they come from every state and must be sponsored by a senator. There are about thirty Senate pages serving every year. Just like the pages who came before them, they go to school early in the morning and work at the Capitol for much of the rest of the day.

"I've been yearning for them to return [after the pandemic] because of their energy, their kindness, and their support," said New Jersey Democratic senator Cory Booker. "They really are part of the groups that make this place run."

Former House pages have fond memories of the program. George W. Andrews III remembered his last day serving as a page in a 2010 interview. He was on the floor of the House

Vice President Marshall with Senate pages on the steps of the Capitol

looking for a member of Congress when he heard a series of bells ringing, which signaled that House business was over for the day. "I'll never forget those four bells ringing that day. And it passed through my mind, 'This is probably the last moment that you will ever be on the House floor when it's in session.' And I can still hear those four bells, loudly and clearly. And I'm glad that I had the sense to appreciate that moment, and I'll always be thankful that I had the opportunity to serve in the United States Congress. It is a magnificent experience."

The program was slow to adapt to change, which may be one reason why it ended in the House. For a long time, there were no people of color or females serving as pages. Technically, the first female page was Gene Cox. She was the thirteen-year-old daughter of a Georgia congressman, and she served just three hours on the job in 1939. At the time it was considered too dangerous for young girls to live and work on their own in a major city. And there was not another female page in the House for more than three decades! There was never a Senate rule specifically forbidding the appointment of women, but deep into the twentieth century, only boys were admitted. In the 1960s, that began to change, and with the Civil Rights Act of 1964 barring discrimination in the workplace, some high school–aged girls began to apply for Senate page appointments. Finally, in 1973, Felda Looper became the first woman to serve as a House page. Speaker

Carl Albert and Felda Looper

of the House Carl Albert of Oklahoma made the historic appointment after receiving a letter from her.

"It was the first time in my life I ever felt discriminated against as a woman, and it made me furious," Looper said when she remembered the moment when she first heard of the unspoken rule that girls could not be pages.

Once it was brought to Albert's attention, he agreed. "The practice of having only male pages in the House is a form of discrimination that should be ended," Albert said.

Just like her male colleagues, Looper's main job was to run errands for members of Congress. "Somebody was going to be first. It was going to happen, and I was psyched it was me," Looper said years later.

American culture in the 1960s was changing, and women and people of color were slowly being given more opportunities, even though some of the older white male members of Congress might have felt threatened and voiced their dissent. The argument that the job would be too physically challenging for girls, or that they could not handle living on their own, was no longer convincing. On the other side of the Capitol, after much debate and stalling, the Senate finally approved a resolution allowing for the appointment of female pages on May 13, 1971. Not long after, Paulette Desell, Ellen McConnell, and Julie Price made Senate history when they were sworn in as the Senate's first female pages.

Paulette Desell-Lund was the first female page in the U.S. Senate, appointed by Senator Jacob Javits of New York. There were logistical issues at the time of her appointment that concerned some. "The notion of—well, the work is too heavy or too hard. What bathrooms would girl pages use? Well, they can't go in the Marble Room—how appropriate is it that they go into the cloakroom?" Desell-Lund recalled. "The concerns about language that the senators might use and what would we wear. Many things that seemed from my perspective as a youngster, foolish nonissues." But she loved the job. "I enjoyed figuring out how to go from here to there. One of the NOT best runs I ever had was when I needed to go to Lowell Weicker's [Republican from Connecticut] office to pick up something and bring it back to the Senate floor. They had not told the cloakroom what it was, so I was sent. I had to pick up a spittoon [a dish made for spitting, used most commonly for people who chew tobacco] for Senator Weicker and bring it back to the Senate floor." When she walked into the cloakroom with the brass spittoon, another page screamed, "Oh God! I can't believe they had you carry that."

The first known Black page in the House was fourteen-year-old Alfred Q. Powell from Manchester, Virginia. He served

Frank Mitchell, the first Black person appointed to the House Page Program in the modern era, is shown with (left to right) Representatives Paul Findley, Leslie Arends, and Gerald Ford.

in the early 1870s, and it was not until 1965 that the House had another Black page. Frank Mitchell was a page during the civil rights movement of the 1960s, and he had a front-row seat during congressional debate about the 1965 Voting Rights Act, legislation that prohibits racial discrimination in voting. The famous civil rights march on Selma, Alabama, had occurred just weeks before his appointment.

"I don't think I broke any barriers for anybody," said Mitchell, who worked in the Republican cloakroom. "But what I did do was carry myself with dignity and respect, and I hope I made it easier for the next guy or woman coming along, so that there wouldn't be any hesitation."

The first Black page in the Senate was Andrew Foote Slade, who served between 1869 and 1881, but his story had been lost to history by the time New York senator Jacob Javits appointed Lawrence Bradford Jr. to be a page in 1965. For decades, Bradford was considered the first Black page, but Slade, whose father, William, worked as a messenger and doorkeeper in the White House and was a confidante of President Abraham Lincoln's, was actually the first.

★ ★ ★

KID HEROES AT THE CAPITOL

Children have always had a presence in the Capitol. Over the years, there have been efforts to honor them. In the 1940s, Congressman Frank Chelf of Kentucky made it his mission to create an award for children who commit acts of bravery. President Truman was the first president to give the award, and now the Young American Medal for Bravery is given to a person eighteen years old or younger who shows "exceptional courage, attended by extraordinary decisiveness, presence of mind, and unusual swiftness of action, regardless of his or her own personal safety, in an effort to save or in saving the life of any person or persons in actual imminent danger." There is a separate Young American Medal for Service for any American eighteen years old or younger "who has achieved outstanding or unusual recognition for character and service during a given calendar year."

Now the awards are presented by the attorney general and not the president. In 1994, Attorney General Janet Reno presented a certificate of commendation to William Thomas Gibbs, whose act of bravery back in 1948 was the one that inspired Congressman Chelf to introduce legislation that created the Young American Medals Program. When he was nine, Mr. Gibbs saved his five-year-old playmate from being hit by a freight train.

Some of the circumstances are incredible and strange: That same year that Reno awarded Gibbs, she also gave the award to Alvin Lee Chapman, of Fort Bridger, Wyoming. That year Alvin, then fourteen, saved his brother, Adam, from an attacking mother otter.

★ ★ ★

The Firsts

There are tremendous firsts that have happened on Capitol Hill over the years, and they are reflections of shifts in the nation. Article I, Section 3 of the U.S. Constitution lists the rules for who can be a senator by saying exactly who cannot be a senator:

"No Person shall be a Senator who shall not have attained to the Age of thirty Years, and been nine Years a Citizen of the United States, and who shall not, when elected, be an Inhabitant of that State for which he shall be chosen."

It was implied that people of color and women need not apply, as they did not have the right to vote during the writing of the constitution. Each one of these firsts are represented by people who had to fight again and again for a seat at the table. In 2021, Congress set a record for the most women

167

and people of color ever being seated, including sixty Black members! The biggest gains have been made in the House of Representatives, where 13 percent of its members are Black. This is almost equal to the percentage of Black people in the United States, according to the Pew Research Center's study of the 117th Congress in January 2021. And although amazing accomplishments have been made, there is still lots of work to be done to get equal representation in Congress for people of color and for women.

In the House, Hispanics are still underrepresented, making up just 9 percent of members. However, 19 percent of the population—or 62 million Americans—identified as Hispanic or Latino in the 2020 census. The same is true for Asian Americans and Pacific Islanders, who, when added together, make up 6 percent of the U.S. population but hold only 3 percent of U.S. House seats. But it is the Senate that is

DID YOU KNOW?

Midterms elections are called that because they are held near the middle of the president's four-year term. The president is not on the ballot, but many governors and members of Congress are.

the furthest behind. Since the Senate first met in 1789, there have been only eleven Black senators.

By voting for people from diverse backgrounds, Americans are making their voices heard. And the firsts, thankfully, keep happening. There were many during the midterm elections held on November 8, 2022.

In 2022, many women and people of color were elected to office for the first time:

Democrat **Becca Balint** became the first woman elected to Congress from Vermont.

Democrat **Summer Lee** was the first Black woman elected to Congress from Pennsylvania.

Republican **Markwayne Mullin** became the first Native American senator from Oklahoma in nearly one hundred years!

Democrat **Shri Thanedar** became the first Indian American elected to Congress from Michigan.

Democrat **Delia Ramirez** was the first Latina elected to Congress from Illinois.

Democrat **Robert Garcia** was elected in California and became the first out LGBTQIA+ immigrant elected to Congress.

Democrat **Alex Padilla** became the first elected Latino senator from California.

Republican **Katie Britt** became the first elected female senator from Alabama.

In 2022, Democratic Representative **Mary Peltola** was sworn in and became the first female member of the U.S. House from Alaska. She is also the first Alaska Native to serve in Congress.

And we can't forget all the firsts that have happened to pave the way for future firsts.

THE FIRST AND ONLY FORMER PRESIDENT TO LATER SERVE AS A MEMBER OF CONGRESS

When he took his seat in the House in 1831, John Quincy Adams, who was the son of John and Abigail Adams, became the only person to return to the House as a representative after being president.

Founding father Alexander Hamilton worried that ex-presidents, after those all-consuming and exciting years in office, would spend their remaining days "wandering among the people like discontented ghosts." Indeed, only two men had post–White House careers that rivaled their time as president: Adams and William Howard Taft, the twenty-seventh president, who was named chief justice of the Supreme Court after he left office. John Quincy had not looked forward to those years after the White House, declaring shortly before leaving office, "There is nothing more pathetic in life than a former president."

When his presidential term was up, he moved into a mansion in Washington, D.C., and wrote, "It was my intention to bury myself in complete retirement as much as any nun taking the veil." Nothing he could do, he thought, would come close to being president. But remarkably, Adams was recruited to run for Congress, even though his wife and son were unimpressed by the prospect. It was an odd idea, after all—a former president becoming a congressman. But Adams was intrigued at the opportunity to step back into public life. On December 5, 1831, he attended the first session of the twenty-second Congress and became the first—and last—former president to do so. Adams considered his new job a major demotion at first.

But Adams enjoyed his new position and the freedom it gave him to speak his mind, even if he was not as powerful as he had once been. And by the end of his eight terms in Congress, he had built a reputation as a leader in the fight against slavery and was known as "Old Man Eloquent"— meaning he talked a lot. It should be noted that as president, he was not an abolitionist or a leader of the antislavery movement. But in Congress, he argued passionately against slavery even amid death threats. "A life devoted to [ending slavery] would be nobly spent or sacrificed," he wrote in his diary. He died in 1848 in the Speaker's Room in the place he grew to love. The way he approached his years as a former president has fascinated men who have left the presidency, but no one has followed his lead yet.

THE FIRST BLACK SENATOR

Have the colored people done anything to justify the prejudice against them that does exist in the hearts of so many white persons and, generally, of one great political party in this country? Have they done anything to justify it? No, sir.

—Hiram R. Revels, during an 1871 debate over school segregation

There have been eleven Black senators since emancipation in 1863, when enslaved people were set free in the states that had seceded from the United States during the Civil War (people were still enslaved in border states). While this is a very low number, it shows the slow evolution from a country built on slavery to one where a descendent of enslaved people can be elected to office. Dr. Martin Luther King Jr. famously said, "We shall overcome because the arc of the moral universe is long, but it bends toward justice." There have been many fits and starts along the way.

As mentioned earlier in this book, Hiram Revels had a

long and fascinating journey to becoming a groundbreaking senator. He was born in Fayetteville, North Carolina, in 1827 to free mixed-race parents, and he was never enslaved, but he experienced racism just the same. It was illegal to educate Black children in North Carolina at the time, so he went to Indiana, where he studied at a Quaker seminary, and later to another seminary for Black students in Ohio.

He was ordained in the African Methodist Episcopal (AME) Church in 1845, and eventually became one of the few Black American men with a college education when he went to Knox College in Galesburg, Illinois, on a scholarship. After the Civil War, in 1866, he and his family settled in Natchez, Mississippi, where a Union general appointed him as an alderman.

Revels was recruited to run for office, and he won a seat in the Mississippi state senate. On January 20, 1870, Revels was selected by the Mississippi state legislature by a vote of eighty-five to fifteen to fill Albert Brown's former seat in the Senate. Revels was one of fifteen Black people who served in Congress during the post–Civil War era. He was elected to fill the vacancy created after the state seceded from the Union before the outbreak of the Civil War.

Revels came to Washington and was met with scattered applause in the gallery, but because Mississippi was not officially readmitted to the United States until a month later, he was kept waiting to do the job he had been elected to do. Not everyone was happy; in fact some members of Congress were furious. There was a group of vocal Senate Democrats who wanted to keep him from serving. They said that because Mississippi was not officially a U.S. state at the time of his appointment, it did not count. The Constitution mandates that a senator must have been a citizen for at least nine years. The Democrats claimed that Revels was not an American citizen until the passage of the Fourteenth Amendment in 1868, and because of that, he was not technically able to run for office. It was an absurd claim, and their efforts to stop him were unsuccessful. Finally, on February 25, 1870, Revels was sworn in as a U.S. senator and the country's first Black member of Congress. He served on the Committee on Education and Labor and the Committee on the District of Columbia. As a former teacher, Revels believed strongly in the value of education, and he spoke out against segregation in schools. He was in office for a year and wrote later of his time in the Senate: "I did all I could for the benefit of my needy and much imposed-upon people."

Revels returned to Mississippi and became the first president of Alcorn State University, a historically Black university. Revels passed away on January 16, 1901. In 1929, Oscar Stanton DePriest, who was from Illinois, became the first Black person to serve in Congress since North Carolina

Senator Hiram R. Revels

representative George H. W. White left the House in 1901. There were no Black members in Congress for the three-decade period before 1929, and in 1963, there were only five.

THE FIRST BLACK MEMBER OF THE HOUSE OF REPRESENTATIVES

[Southern Democrats], sir, would not give to the colored man the right to vote or the right to enjoy any

of those immunities which are enjoyed by other citizens, if it had a tendency to make him feel his manhood and elevate him above the ordinary way of life. So long as he makes himself content with ordinary gifts, why it is all well; but when he aspires to be a man, when he seeks to have the rights accorded him that other citizens of the country enjoy, then he is asking too much, and such gentlemen as the gentleman from Kentucky are not willing to grant it.

—Joseph Rainey in a speech before Congress, December 19, 1873

Several months after Hiram Revels was sworn in, Joseph Rainey became the first Black person to serve in the House of Representatives, and he served for a decade. Joseph Hayne Rainey was born on June 21, 1832, in Georgetown, South Carolina. As noted earlier, he was the first member of Congress who was born into enslavement. His parents were enslaved, but his father worked as a barber, and he was able to keep a small share of his income. In the early 1840s, he used part of those wages to buy his family their freedom. Still, Rainey could not attend school because Black people were not allowed to. But Rainey followed in his father's footsteps and became a barber and an entrepreneur. His business— Rainey's Hair Cutting Salon—was located at the Mills House Hotel in Charleston, South Carolina.

Representative Joseph H. Rainey

Abraham Lincoln won the 1860 presidential election, and that same year, members of the South Carolina legislature voted unanimously to leave the Union. By 1866, there were 400,000 newly freed people in the state. The free Black population was now in the majority, and they used peaceful protests, including sit-ins, to claim their rights as American citizens.

Rainey decided politics was the best way to help freed Black people gain access to the rights deserved by every citizen. He worked in Republican state politics, and in 1868 won the election to the South Carolina state senate, where he served as chairman of the Finance Committee. In July, he cast his vote in the General Assembly to ratify the Fourteenth Amendment, which gave full citizenship to all people born in America, including the formerly enslaved. Black Americans now had "equal protection of the laws." They were still discriminated against, however, and were far from truly free.

Rainey was nominated to the House of Representatives by the Republican Party to fill the seat of a congressman from South Carolina who had been accused of illegal conduct. On November 8, 1870, when he ran for a full term, he won with more than 86 percent of the vote. Rainey was sworn in on December 12, 1870, as the first Black U.S. representative. It was on April 29, 1874, that Rainey also became the first Black American to preside over the House of Representatives from the Speaker's chair as Speaker pro tempore during a debate.

Rainey worked tirelessly to protect the four million formerly enslaved people who were under siege from violence in the South. He was an eloquent speaker, and on April 1, 1871, he delivered a powerful speech on the House floor in support of the Ku Klux Klan Act. The bill called for the president to stop states in the former Confederacy from denying "any person or any class of persons of the equal protection of the laws, or of equal privileges or immunities under the laws." Essentially, he was asking for an end to discrimination by shining a spotlight on injustice and violence against people of color as someone who had experienced racism firsthand.

Rainey spoke in support of Republican senator Charles Sumner, an abolitionist from Massachusetts, and his bill to eliminate racial discrimination in juries, schools, and other areas crucial to civic life. Rainey's first priority in office was always protecting the four million formerly enslaved people whose ranks he had once been among. He also spoke in support of the sovereignty of Native American tribes and for the human rights and economic interests of every American citizen.

Rainey was ahead of his time. Not only did he fight for civil rights, but he also took on the issue of election fraud after threats of violence against Republican voters and Black people living in South Carolina were threatening the already shaky peace in the post–Civil War Southern states. Rainey himself was the target of white supremacists, and he asked for federal troops to help protect him. Rainey served for more than eight years and dedicated his work to furthering civil rights. "I can only raise my voice," Rainey said in 1877, "and I would do it if it were the last time I ever did it, in defense of my rights and in the interests of my oppressed people." In 1878, Rainey was defeated by Democrat John S. Richardson, a former Confederate officer, with almost 62 percent of the vote. Rainey eventually left Washington and moved back to Georgetown, South Carolina. He died on August 1, 1887.

In 2005, an oil painting of Rainey was unveiled on Capitol Hill. And in February 2022, 144 years after Rainey left Congress, he was honored with a room bearing his name in the Capitol. His great-granddaughter Lorna Rainey was at the ceremony. "This is not a Black story or a white story," she said. "This is a story of inspiration, of courage, of forward thinking." Studying the mistakes of the past helps us learn how not to repeat them, and studying the brave people who were pathfinders and trailblazers gives us appreciation for progress, even when it is not nearly enough.

THE FIRST HISPANIC AMERICAN REPRESENTATIVE

José Antonio Romualdo Pacheco Jr. was born on October 31, 1831, in Santa Barbara, California, when the state was still a Mexican territory. His mother was from a wealthy Mexican family, and his father, a captain in the Mexican army, was killed shortly after his birth. Pacheco and his older brother went to school in Honolulu, Hawaii, and when he returned home, he worked with his stepfather and helped manage his parents' estates in Southern California.

Pacheco's family was very involved in politics and committed to protecting the rights of landowners like themselves. His stepfather and his brother were both state politicians,

and Pacheco began his political career as a superior court
judge for San Luis Obispo
County from 1853 to 1857.
He then became a state
senator until 1862. He
first ran as a Democrat but
switched parties and became
a Republican. In 1863, he was
appointed as state treasurer because of a

FUN FACT

Pacheco was an experienced rancher and to date, he is the only California governor known to have actually lassoed a grizzly bear.

vacancy, and a year later, he won election for an entire term.
In 1871, he was nominated to be lieutenant governor, and
became the governor of California in 1875. He was the first
Hispanic American and the first native Californian to serve
as governor.

Pacheco ran for a U.S. House seat in 1876. He appealed to
the majority-Hispanic population who valued his experience
as a rancher growing up in a state that was considered a
frontier at the time. He took the oath of office on October
17, 1877, after a hard-fought election. He reportedly won by
a single vote! He was the first Hispanic member with full
voting rights.

Pacheco was eventually unseated, but he ran for a House
seat again in 1878 and was a member of Congress until 1883.
He campaigned in English and Spanish. He worked to protect

Representative Romualdo Pacheco

the rights of landowners in his Californian district while also helping expand the area's commerce by improving and expanding harbors and railroads. The Republican leadership installed him as chairman of the Committee on Private Land Claims in 1881, which made him the first Hispanic member to chair a full committee.

Pacheco did not run for reelection in 1882. Instead, he went home to California and continued his career in business. He passed away on January 23, 1899. His *Los Angeles Times* obituary read, "We have public men who might well copy in some measure the pose of mind, the calm dignity, the graceful honesty and gentle manliness of Romualdo Pacheco."

THE FIRST ASIAN AMERICAN REPRESENTATIVE

Dalip Singh Saund was born in 1899 in the northern province of Punjab, India, which was a British colony at the time. He graduated from the University of the Punjab with a degree in mathematics. He came to the United States in 1920 and studied at the University of California, Berkeley.

He sought to learn about food canning with a plan to return to India with his new skill set as soon as he could. Berkeley, California, was not an easy place to live for Indian and Asian students, and "outside of the university atmosphere," he later wrote, "it was made quite evident that people from Asia— Japanese, Chinese, and Hindus—were not wanted." Saund earned master's and PhD degrees in mathematics.

Saund became especially inspired by Abraham Lincoln and particularly the Gettysburg Address. Lincoln, he said, changed the course of his life. "Even though life for me did not seem very easy, it had become impossible to think of life separated from the United States," he wrote in his autobiography, *Congressman from India*. "The only way Indians in California could make a living at that time was to join with others who had settled in various parts of the state as farmers." He settled in Southern California, where a friend offered him a job as the foreman of a group of farmworkers. He got involved in local politics, wanting to help Indian immigrants like himself.

Saund worked to lift restrictions prohibiting people born in India from becoming U.S. citizens. His efforts were successful, and in 1949 he became a U.S. citizen. He was a businessman and a county judge in Southern California. He ran for a seat in the House and won in 1956, becoming the first person of Asian descent elected to Congress. He won despite the racism he experienced as his opponents pointed out again and again that he was not born in the United States, and even made fun of the turban he wore. It was a tremendous victory; his congressional district was geographically larger "than Massachusetts, Rhode Island, and Delaware combined" according to the *New York Times*. But the race was not easy. His Republican opponent was decorated female army pilot Jacqueline Cochran Odlum. Because the candidates were different from usual, the race became national news. "A woman's 'smoldering hope' and the success story of an East Indian immigrant are converging into what is likely to be one of the most colorful Congressional contests of 1956," reported the *New York Times*. "Seldom if ever has the American melting pot cooked up a spicier election dish than the contest now simmering in California's 29th Congressional District," wrote the *Los Angeles Times*. So Saund faced racism in the media as well. But because Saund was a farmer who knew firsthand the struggles other farmers were facing, and because he knew the area so well, he convinced voters in his district that he would work hard for them. He won about 52 percent of the vote.

He dedicated the rest of his life to helping the residents of his district, including helping veterans get access to benefits, getting funding for irrigation projects to help farmers, and building new post offices and roads. He was starting his campaign for a fourth term when, in May 1962, he suffered a severe stroke. He died on April 22, 1973.

After his death, he was praised by his colleagues, including Majority Leader Tip O'Neill of Massachusetts. "To chronicle all his legislative achievements and personal successes during his lifetime could not begin to pay Dalip Saund the justice and honor he deserves," O'Neill said. "Those of us who knew and admired him in the House, remember him as a man of boundless energy, personal integrity, and strong convictions—consistently and tirelessly fighting for the right of 'life, liberty, and the pursuit of happiness' for all Americans."

Representative Dalip Singh Saund

THE YEAR OF THE WOMAN

A turning point for women's representation in Congress came in 1992, when four women were elected to the Senate in just one year. This became known as "the Year of the Woman." This may not seem like such a big deal, but at the time, there were only two female senators: Barbara Mikulski, a Democrat from Maryland, and Nancy Kassebaum, a Republican from Kansas. The four women who won in 1992 were Patty Murray of Washington, Dianne Feinstein and Barbara Boxer of California, and Carol Moseley Braun of Illinois. Part of their inspiration to run came from the sexism they saw during the Senate confirmation hearings for Supreme Court nominee Clarence Thomas, who was accused by Anita Hill of sexual harassment.

"Calling 1992 the Year of the Woman makes it sound like the Year of the Caribou or the Year of the Asparagus," said Senator Mikulski, who became the first woman elected to statewide office in Maryland when she became a senator in 1986. "We're not a fad, a fancy, or a year."

Counting both the House of Representatives and the Senate, women account for 153 of 540 voting and nonvoting members of Congress in the 118th Congress in 2023. That's a 59 percent increase from the ninety-six women who were in Congress a decade ago. Though it's still below women's share of the population, it shows real progress.

But it all began somewhere, and here are a few firsts by important women who helped start it all.

THE FIRST WOMAN TO SERVE IN CONGRESS

I may be the first woman member of Congress, but I won't be the last.
—Jeannette Rankin when she won her congressional seat in the 1916 election

Jeannette Rankin was born outside Missoula, Montana, in 1880. She was the oldest of six siblings and came from a prominent wealthy family at a time when girls were expected to put tending to their sisters and brothers above their schoolwork. Back then, a woman's name was to appear in print three times in her life: her birth, her marriage announcement, and her obituary. But Rankin's family was different.

Her parents recognized Jeannette's intelligence and fostered her education. She graduated from Montana State University with a degree in biology in 1902, when very few women attended college. And instead of getting married and having children, she became an activist. In 1908, she moved to New York City to get a degree in social work from the first graduate social work program. The school was located near the Lower East Side, where there was lots of poverty. The experience made her see how important it was for women to have the right to vote. "I saw that if we were to have decent laws for children, sanitary jails, safe food supplies, women would have to vote," she said.

She fought for white women's right to vote, known as suffrage, all over the country. She was not concerned with voting rights for women of color, and her record shows an activist whose views were limited in scope.

Jeannette was a gifted public speaker, and she made a career as a lobbyist for the National American Woman Suffrage Association. She helped put together the New York Women's Suffrage Party, and in 1911, she was the first woman to make a passionate speech for women's suffrage before the Montana state legislature. In 1914, Montana granted white women voting rights and the right to run for office. Indigenous women were not given the same right until 1924. In New Mexico, members of Indigenous tribes did not get the right to vote in state elections until 1948.

Rankin took the bold move of running for office. On April 2, 1917, when she was thirty-six years old, she became the first woman ever sworn in as a member of Congress. She used her skills as an activist to rally support from newly enfranchised women voters, and she campaigned around her district on horseback. "I knew the women would stand by me. The women worked splendidly, and I am sure they feel that the results have been worth the effort," she said

Congresswoman Jeannette Rankin

in a statement. "I am deeply conscious of the responsibility, and it is wonderful to have the opportunity to be the first woman to sit in Congress. I will not only represent the women of Montana, but also the women of the country, and I have plenty of work cut out for me."

DID YOU KNOW?

Even as 1920 marked a turning point that gave most white women the right to vote, many women of color were still disenfranchised, or not given the right to vote. That was because of a series of state laws that kept Black Americans from voting by adding extra requirements, including the ability to explain parts of the State Constitution, poll taxes, and the rise of Jim Crow laws. All those elements combined with the threat of violence meant that many Black Americans, men and women, did not get the right to vote in 1920.

Rankin was a famous pacifist who did not believe in war under any circumstances. "You can no more win a war than you can win an earthquake," she said. On her first day in office, President Woodrow Wilson asked Congress to vote to declare war against Germany, which would mark the nation's entrance into World War I. Instead of simply saying "yea" or "nay" to indicate her vote, Rankin broke a 140-year-old precedent and stood up to explain her vote. "I wish to stand for my country," she said, "but I cannot stand for war."

She also ran as a pacifist as the country was on the brink of entering World War II. In 1941, she returned to Congress and was one of only nine women serving. On December 8, 1941, the day after the Japanese attack on Pearl Harbor, Franklin Delano Roosevelt came to the joint session of Congress to make his case that a state of war already existed after the attack. Rankin voted against the U.S. declaration of war against Japan. She was the only member of Congress to do so.

After she cast that very controversial vote, she issued this statement: "As a woman, I can't go to war, and I refuse to send anyone else." Loud boos erupted, and she had to hide in a phone booth, where she called security and waited for a guard to bring her to safety.

This time her vote and her unshakable commitment to pacifism ended her political career. But she continued working as a political activist, and during the Vietnam War, when she was eighty-eight years old, she led a march of five thousand women in Washington, D.C., to protest the war. The marchers called themselves the Jeannette Rankin Brigade. Rankin would not stay silent; she spoke on the steps of the Capitol and declared: "The world must finally understand that we cannot settle disputes by eliminating human beings."

She remained an antiwar and women's rights activist until she passed away in 1973, when she was ninety-two years old. Her statue is in the U.S. Capitol. As of 2023, Montana has not elected a woman to Congress since Rankin.

THE FIRST WOMAN TO BE ELECTED TO THE SENATE

Hattie Ophelia Wyatt Caraway was only supposed to be a senator for a few months. When her husband, Arkansas Democratic senator Thaddeus Caraway, passed away in November 1931, party leaders needed a stand-in until the special election. What they did not bet on was that Hattie, who was fifty-four years old at the time, was interested in politics and was not content to simply be a seat holder.

A lot of people made fun of her for thinking she could win, but they underestimated the fierceness of the "little

Senator Hattie W. Caraway

lady from Arkansas." On January 12, 1932, she beat two male opponents to become the first woman elected to the Senate. Then she was reelected in 1938, and served as a senator until 1945. When she decided to run for office the first time, she wrote in her diary: "If I can hold on to my sense of humor and a modicum of dignity I shall have a wonderful time running for office, whether I get there or not."

Caraway saw herself as a voice for the common man and woman in Arkansas. She was nicknamed Silent Hattie because, unlike many of her colleagues, she did not like to give long-winded speeches. But she tried to help people in Arkansas when she could. A saying in the state went something like this: "Write Senator Caraway. She will help you if she can."

Her male colleagues were not very welcoming, but on her last day in the Senate in 1945, Caraway received a standing ovation.

THE FIRST WOMAN OF COLOR AND THE FIRST ASIAN AMERICAN WOMAN ELECTED TO CONGRESS

On December 6, 1927, Patsy Matsu Takemoto was born in Paia, Hawaii, before Hawaii became a state. During World War II, when the United States was at war with Japan, Japanese Americans were treated terribly. Their property was confiscated, and they were sent to prison without trial. Patsy was a fierce opponent of discrimination, which she experienced firsthand, and she became interested in politics from a young age. When she was a junior in high school, she launched her first student government campaign and won class president. After she graduated as valedictorian in 1944, she went to college in Pennsylvania and Nebraska but suffered racial discrimination. Because she was a student of color, she could not live in the same place as the white students. She transferred to the University of Hawaii and studied medicine, graduating in 1948.

Patsy applied to medical school but was not accepted, and she was even told that she was denied entry because she was a woman. She decided to apply to the University of Chicago Law School, where she graduated as one of two women in her class in 1951. She got married and had a baby and again faced discrimination when she had trouble finding a job because she was a woman, and also because she was in an interracial marriage. Like the other firsts, she did not let adversity stop her. She went on to become the first Japanese American woman to practice law in Hawaii. She also founded the Oahu Young Democrats in 1954, and as soon as Hawaii became the fiftieth state in 1959, she set her sights on becoming an elected representative.

While Mink lost her first election, she ran again in 1962 and won a seat in the Hawaii state senate. In 1964 she won a seat in the U.S. House of Representatives, making her the first woman of color and the first Asian American woman to serve in Congress. She was one of the key authors and supporters of Title IX, a law that helped further women's athletic opportunities by barring sexual discrimination in institutions that receive federal funds. Title IX transformed women's athletics forever. It states that "no person in the United States shall, on the basis of sex, be excluded from participation in, be denied the benefits of, or be subjected to discrimination under any education program or activity receiving Federal financial assistance."

Patsy made the long journey from Washington, D.C., back to Hawaii every other week to check in with the people who elected her. She ran for president in 1972 as part of her efforts to draw attention to the antiwar movement. She was the first Asian American to run for the highest office in the land, and even though she lost, it was a groundbreaking campaign. Mink worked to promote racial and gender equality in schools, and in 1974 she got the Women's Educational Equity Act passed.

In 1976, she ran for a seat in the Senate, but she lost. She stayed active in Democratic politics in Hawaii and was elected to the Honolulu city council, where she served from 1983 to 1987. Like Jeannette Rankin, she ran for a House seat later

Congresswoman Patsy Takemoto Mink

in life, and was reelected in 1990, when she ran on the campaign slogan "The Experience of a Lifetime," touting her earlier years serving in Congress. She served another six terms and continued to fight on behalf of women and people of color, particularly Asian Pacific Americans. She worked with colleagues in forming the Congressional Asian Pacific American Caucus in 1994 and she went on to chair the committee. "We have felt that we have not been consulted on important steps taken by this administration and ones in the past," Mink argued.

In total she served for a remarkable twelve terms in Congress, working on education and health care legislation.

She saw herself as a representative of her race and gender. She said she knew that "because there were only eight women at the time who were Members of Congress, that I had a special burden to bear to speak for [all women], because they didn't have people who could express their concerns for them adequately. So, I always felt that we were serving a dual role in Congress, representing our own districts and, at the same time, having to voice the concerns of the total population of women in the country."

In September 2002, Mink passed away in her beloved Honolulu, Hawaii. But because the election was in November, her name was still on the ballot, and she won by a wide margin. She was replaced by Ed Case. The Title IX law was renamed the Patsy T. Mink Equal Opportunity in Education Act after her death. In 2014, she was posthumously awarded the Presidential Medal of Freedom, the highest civilian honor in the country.

Her colleague and cofounder of the Congressional Asian Pacific American Caucus, Norman Mineta, a Democrat from California, called Mink "an American hero, a leader and a trailblazer who made an irreplaceable mark in the fabric of our country." Mink's daughter, Wendy, said, "I am the child of someone who made a huge difference for women and girls in education. She taught me change might be slow, but change is going to happen."

THE FIRST BLACK FEMALE REPRESENTATIVE

Shirley Chisholm was born in 1924 in Brooklyn, New York, the daughter of immigrants. Her father was a factory worker from Guyana, and her mother was a seamstress from Barbados. She excelled in school and worked as a teacher and a director of day care centers before advising New York City as an educational consultant. In 1964, she was elected to the state legislature and became the second Black woman to hold the office.

When she decided to run for Congress, Chisholm threw all her time and passion into her campaign. She would pull up to apartment buildings in a truck with a loudspeaker and announce, "Ladies and gentlemen . . . this is fighting Shirley Chisholm coming through." Chisholm capitalized on her personal campaign style. "I have a way of talking that does something to people," she said. "I have a theory about campaigning. You have to let them feel you."

Her signature campaign slogan, "Unbought and unbossed," which was later the title of her autobiography, carried a powerful message: she ran without the support of the Brooklyn Democratic Party and she held herself accountable only to the voters. Her top priorities were raising incomes for working people, commanding respect for Black people and women, and getting more money for public education.

Congresswoman Shirley Chisholm

When she won her race to represent New York's Twelfth Congressional District in 1968 and became the first Black woman elected to Congress, she was asked how she felt about being the first. "Actually," she said bluntly, "it's overdue, so I don't get terribly excited about it."

She wasted no time speaking up for herself. When she first got to Congress, she spoke on the House floor and protested her assignment to the Committee on Agriculture. She was told by a longtime congressman that she should be a "good soldier," but she demanded a more relevant assignment for her urban district, and she got it. When she was reassigned to the Committee on Veterans' Affairs, she said, "There are a lot more veterans in my district than trees."

She became the first Black American to seek the Democratic Party's presidential nomination when she ran in 1972. Even though she did not win, her outspoken personality and commitment to being the voice for the people in her district made her one of the ten most-admired women in America according to a 1974 Gallup poll.

Chisholm spent fourteen years in Congress and cofounded the Congressional Black Caucus and the Congressional Women's Caucus. She left Congress in January 1983 and cofounded the National Congress of Black Women. She passed away on January 1, 2005, at eighty years old.

In 2015, President Barack Obama posthumously awarded her the Presidential Medal of Freedom. "Shirley Chisholm's example transcends her life," he said. "And when asked how she'd like to be remembered, she had an answer: 'I'd like them to say that Shirley Chisholm had guts.' And I'm proud to say it: Shirley Chisholm had guts."

THE FIRST HISPANIC AMERICAN WOMAN TO SERVE IN THE HOUSE

Ileana Ros-Lehtinen was born in Havana, Cuba, on July 15, 1952, and came to the United States when she was eight years old, not long after Fidel Castro took power. In 1982, she was elected to the Florida House of Representatives, becoming the first Hispanic woman to be elected to the Florida state legislature. In 1986, she became a state senator, and in 1989, she became the first Hispanic woman ever elected to the U.S. House of Representatives.

Ros-Lehtinen actually learned that she was the first Hispanic congresswoman when journalist Katie Couric asked her how it felt in an interview on the *Today* show.

Congresswoman Ileana Ros-Lehtinen

Ros-Lehtinen felt tremendous pressure to speak for all Hispanic women who had not had a voice. "I always felt a great sense of obligation, that I was representing not just the Cuban American community but women as well, and Latina women especially. I've always felt that burden, that responsibility, and that privilege to be a voice greater than myself. And that does not mean that all Latinas agree with me or that all women agree with me or that all Cuban Americans agree with me. I don't mean that at all. But by and large, I try to speak on behalf of a greater number of people so that folks feel like they're represented here in the United States Congress."

She focused on education and also on relations with Cuba as a member of the Foreign Affairs Committee. She was the first woman to ever chair that important House panel. She served for thirty years—an amazing fifteen terms!—and retired in 2019. She understood it was time to leave and let a younger generation take over with their own ideas.

"There was no epiphany. There was no moment, nothing that has happened that I've said, 'I've got to move on,'" she reflected. "It was just a realization that I could keep getting elected—but it's not about getting elected."

THE FIRST WOMAN TO SERVE AS SPEAKER OF THE HOUSE

Nancy Pelosi was born in Baltimore, Maryland, in 1940 into a large Italian American Catholic family with strong ties to the Democratic Party. She grew up with five older brothers, and she was the only girl in the family. Her father, Thomas D'Alesandro Jr., was mayor of Baltimore for twelve years, and before that, he represented the city for five terms in the U.S. House. Her brother also served as mayor of Baltimore. She graduated from Trinity College in Washington, D.C.

Pelosi grew up in the Little Italy section of Baltimore, and as a young girl she listened as her father talked about his work in politics, and she developed a keen sense of politics and power. She learned by watching her father figure out his path to win election after election. She realized early on something that helped guide her own path to become the most powerful woman in American politics during her lifetime: "Power's not anything that anybody gives away," she said. "You have to fight for it."

Nancy Pelosi has represented her district of San Francisco, California, in Congress for more than three decades. She has been in charge of getting House Democrats elected for two decades, and she has served as House Democratic whip, the person who counts votes and makes sure that members of the party stick together.

Speaker Nancy Pelosi

One of the ways she rose to prominence was by forging relationships with powerful Democrats and becoming a very energetic fundraiser for her party. She is especially proud of her work to pass the Affordable Care Act, health care reform enacted when Barack Obama was president. She recognizes what her speakership represents for women around the country. "Nothing is more important than the full involvement of women in decision-making in our society, whether it is governmental, education, military, corporate America, so my message to young women would be: know your power, be confident, and understand that nothing is more important than you fulfilling your role, whatever that may be."

But what Nancy Pelosi is most known for is becoming the first woman ever to serve as Speaker of the House in 2007, which made her the highest-ranking woman in U.S. history at that time. The Speaker is second only to the vice president in the line of succession, which determines who becomes president if the president is no longer able to serve. The Speaker is the political leader of the House, and when Pelosi became Speaker, she became the most powerful Democrat, next to the president, in the country.

"It's a historic moment for the Congress, it's a historic moment for the women of America," she said when she became Speaker. "It is a moment for which we have waited over two hundred years. Never losing faith, we waited through the many years of struggle to achieve our rights. But women weren't just waiting, women were working, never losing faith we worked to redeem the promise of America that all men, and women, are created equal. . . . For our daughters and our granddaughters now the sky is the limit, anything is possible for them."

In 2023, Pelosi stepped down as speaker after Republicans won the majority of House seats. "Your path is your path, don't worry about following somebody else's path. It will have its own natural tempo."

THE FIRST WOMAN ELECTED TO BOTH HOUSES OF CONGRESS

Margaret Madeline Chase was born in Skowhegan, Maine, in 1897. She was the oldest of six children. Her father was a barber and her mother held several jobs, including working as a store clerk and a server in a restaurant. Chase followed in her mother's footsteps and worked a lot herself, and after graduating from high school, she worked as a reporter at a local newspaper. In 1930, she married Clyde Harold Smith, who was elected to the House of Representatives in 1936.

Clyde got sick in 1940, and it was decided that he might not be able to survive another campaign, so he asked his wife to run in his place. The end of his career was the beginning of hers. She won the Republican special primary held to fill his unexpired term, beating her Democratic challenger. She then won a full term herself, and was Maine's first female member of Congress.

She was reelected to the House for several terms, and she announced that she was

> **FUN FACT**
>
> For decades, there was no women's bathroom close to the Senate floor. A women's restroom was finally opened near the floor in 1992, when fifty-four women were elected to Congress. There were only thirty-four women serving in Congress in 1991, so that represents a 58.8 percent leap in the number of women lawmakers.

running for the Senate in 1947 to take the place of a retiring senator. She was a natural campaigner, and some of her constituents were so comfortable with her that they called her Margaret. She had a crew of dedicated women who campaigned for her across the state, and she won her Senate seat in a landslide, which made her the very first woman ever elected to the House and the Senate.

She was reelected to the Senate three more times. She became used to being the only woman in a room where important decisions were made.

Like Shirley Chisholm, Smith was going to take on the issues she wanted to, not those that were expected from a woman during her time. She was actively involved in military affairs as the first woman to serve on the prestigious Senate Committee on Armed Services. She was also very interested in post–World War II reconstruction, and she was worried about the threat of Communism from Eastern Europe. But she was strongly opposed to the House Un-American Activities Committee and Wisconsin senator Joseph McCarthy, a fellow Republican, who was exposing people suspected of Communist ties (whether they had them or not) and destroying their lives. Even when her own Republican Party was largely supportive or silent, Smith denounced McCarthy and his Red Scare, a period in history discussed earlier, when there was a climate of fear about Communism that led to censorship.

She spent more than three decades in Congress, and she was not afraid to speak out against members of her own political party if she disagreed with them. "Freedom of speech," she said, "is not what it used to be in America. It has been so abused by some that it is not exercised by others." Only six other Republican senators joined Smith in voicing their outrage about McCarthy and the threat he presented to democracy.

Smith announced that she would run for president in January 1964. "I have few illusions and no money, but I'm staying for the finish," she noted. "When people keep telling you, you can't do a thing, you kind of like to try." She approached the campaign for president as she had her many campaigns for Congress and relied on grassroots support. She lost every primary, but she accomplished something no one else had: at the 1964 Republican Convention, she became the first woman to have her name put in for nomination for the presidency by a major political party. Despite receiving the support of just twenty-seven delegates and losing the nomination to Senate colleague Barry Goldwater, it was a symbolic achievement.

In 1972, she lost her fifth campaign for the Senate.

When she left office, Smith went back home to Skowhegan. She spent her time working on the development of the Margaret Chase Smith Library Center, the first library devoted to the papers of a female member of Congress. While she might not have sought praise during her years in Congress, she wanted the women who would follow in her footsteps to learn from her successes and mistakes. In 1989, President George H. W. Bush awarded her the Presidential Medal of Freedom. Bush honored her years in Congress, saying: "She looked beyond the politics of the time to see the future of America, and made us all better for it."

Congresswoman Margaret Chase Smith, U.S. Representative and U.S. Senator

On May 29, 1995, at the age of ninety-seven, Smith died in her hometown. In June 2022, a room in the Capitol building was dedicated to Smith and to Maryland senator Barbara Mikulski, a Democrat, who held the record of the longest-serving woman in Congress until Democrat Marcy Kaptur won her twenty-first term in the House in 2022. They are the first female senators to have rooms dedicated to them.

LGBTQIA+ REPRESENTATION IN CONGRESS

Since the 1970s, openly gay candidates have been winning elected office, but their numbers used to be small. Today, according to the LGBTQIA+ Victory Fund, there are more than one thousand LGBTQIA+ people in elected office in the United States, which is a record.

Thirteen members of the 118th Congress, which convened on January 3, 2023, openly identify as lesbian, gay, or bisexual, according to a Pew Research Center analysis. This is the highest number in American history! They are still underrepresented, however, when you look at their share in the greater U.S. population, which according to a 2021 Gallup survey, is at least 6.5 percent. The thirteen members of Congress who identify as lesbian, gay, or bisexual made up only 2 percent of the 534 voting lawmakers as of January 3, 2023. But many have paved a path going forward, and here are a few of those firsts.

THE FIRST MEMBER OF CONGRESS TO VOLUNTARILY COME OUT AS GAY

Barney Frank was first elected to Congress as a Democrat from Massachusetts in 1981, and he spent three decades in Congress, retiring in 2013. When he was a state legislator, he introduced Massachusetts's first gay rights bill in 1972. This was during a time when laws were in place that denied gay people opportunities and basic rights.

In 1987, at forty-seven years old, Frank told the press that he was gay. "If you ask the direct question: 'Are you gay?' the answer is yes. So what?" Mr. Frank told the *Boston*

Globe. "I've said all along that if I was asked by a reporter and I didn't respond it would look like I had something to hide, and I don't think I have anything to hide." In 2015, he wrote about his anguished and conflicted feelings before he revealed his sexuality. "For many years, I was ashamed of myself for hiding my membership in a universally despised group. I'd been afraid

Congressman Barney Frank

of exposure, and angry at myself for my self-denial."

It was something no member of Congress had ever done before. But he blames himself for not being even bolder and doing it sooner. "I should have come out a little earlier," he said in a 2020 interview.

Frank's legislative legacy includes his push for stricter regulations and more protections for consumers in the banking industry. But it was what he did to change American culture and reduce the stigma surrounding homosexuality at the time that brought the most lasting change.

Back in 1987, he explained how he felt about his decision. He said that while he did not think that his personal life had anything to do with his job, "I don't want to leave the impression that I'm embarrassed about my life."

THE FIRST OPENLY GAY PERSON TO BE ELECTED TO THE SENATE

Tammy Baldwin was born in 1962 in Madison, Wisconsin, and was raised by her grandparents. Her grandfather worked as a scientist at the University of Wisconsin–Madison and her grandmother was the head costumer of the University of Wisconsin–Madison Theater Department. Tammy's mother struggled with addiction and mental illness and was unable to take care of her. Baldwin was nine years old when she got sick with an illness that required hospitalization. Her grandparents had health insurance, but because she was their grandchild, it did not cover her three-month-long stay in the hospital. This personal experience made her want to support health care reform and eventually helped launch her public crusade to help get health care coverage to more people.

Her experience in student government as a middle schooler made her realize that she "could make a difference." After high school, she majored in political science and mathematics at Smith College. "I started working on other people's campaigns," she said, "and following what was happening in local government, and thought, 'I could make a difference again.'" She went back home to Wisconsin and got her law degree from the University of Wisconsin Law School.

In 1986, when she was just twenty-four years old, Tammy

Baldwin was elected to local office, and in 1999 she became the first gay woman and the first openly LGBTQIA+ nonincumbent elected to Congress. In 2012, she became the first openly LGBTQIA+ person elected to the Senate. "It shattered a glass ceiling that hadn't been shattered before," she said in a 2014 interview. "Frankly, the same is true of my becoming the first woman ever elected from the state of Wisconsin to Congress."

It was not always easy to be honest about who she was. At the time, fewer than 1 percent of elected officials in the United States identified as LGBTQIA+. "I really worried that I might have this choice between being honest about who I am and running for office, like I had hoped to do to make change. I remember the time and the moment where I realized I could have both," Baldwin recalled. "I could be totally honest about who I am, and I can run for office, and I can win. What it was for me is a very freeing moment."

Senator Tammy Baldwin

As a member of Congress, Baldwin has worked to support LGBTQIA+ rights and has spoken out in favor of stricter gun control legislation. "Voters see immediately if you're authentic or if you're hiding something, if you have integrity or you're parsing your words too carefully," she said. Being honest and authentic, she added, "can even be viewed as an asset or an advantage from that perspective of courage, integrity and honesty."

FIRST OPENLY GAY PERSON OF COLOR IN CONGRESS

Like Senator Tammy Baldwin, Mark Takano is proud of making history, but he would like to be known as a "substantive legislator" first and someone who also happens to be Japanese American and gay second.

> *More diversity in Congress will produce better outcomes.*
> —Mark Takano

Takano remembers watching the televised Watergate hearing in Congress when he was thirteen years old. This was the famous political scandal involving President Richard Nixon. Takano was mesmerized by what he saw. He especially admired the questions from Congresswoman Barbara Jordan, a Black Democrat from Texas. Takano said, "She was an example of a minority in the highest levels of government." Watching her on television, he said, "opened a sense of possibility for me." He considered that moment to be "the birth" of his "ambition."

Takano was born in Riverside, California, in 1960. Decades earlier, his Japanese American grandparents and parents were ordered by the federal government to leave their Riverside homes and were placed in internment camps during World War II.

Representative Mark Takano

They were jailed without any representation, but they had committed no crime other than being of Japanese descent when the United States was fighting a war against Japan. Like many other Japanese Americans, Takano's family lost everything and had to start all over once they were finally released.

Takano was valedictorian when he graduated from La Sierra High School in 1979. He attended Harvard and then enrolled in the University of California, Riverside, where he earned a teaching degree. In 1987, he started teaching British literature, and he ran for the board of trustees of Riverside Community College District in 1990. He became president of the group shortly after. In 1992, he ran and lost his race for Congress. In keeping with the other firsts, he did not take no for an answer, and he ran again in 1994. He lost the election and continued teaching—never losing sight of his ambition to run for office.

More than ten years went by. It was a group of students who asked him to help form a Gay-Straight Alliance at their school shortly after the 2008 election that renewed his desire to run for office. At that time, California voters had recently passed Proposition 8, which struck down marriage equality in the state. (Shortly after, the ban was overturned by the courts.) "When Prop 8 passed in California, it energized a group of students. I didn't know them and I didn't know what to do with the group . . . but I couldn't let them down," Takano recalled. "The students were, by and large, my inspiration for rethinking things."

Takano, who was then fifty-one years old, ran in 2012 with the support of Representative Barney Frank of Massachusetts. He beat his opponent by more than 17 percent. He was open and proud of being gay and of his support for LGBTQIA+ rights. Once in office, he was determined to tackle other issues he cared about, including education and climate change.

"The significance of that achievement is the unique voice that an openly gay person of color and member of Congress can bring to the House floor and the House committee rooms," Takano said in an interview with the *Washington Blade.* "It's a double-awareness of what it means to be vulnerable."

FIRST OPENLY GAY WOMAN OF COLOR IN CONGRESS

Born in 1980 and raised by a single mother who was a member of the U.S. Army, Sharice Davids broke many glass ceilings when she was first elected to Congress in 2018. She is the first openly gay woman of color in the House, the first openly gay person elected to represent Kansas in Congress, and one of the first two Indigenous women ever elected to Congress. She is a member of the Ho-Chunk Nation of Wisconsin.

Davids's mother served in the army for two decades, and Davids was the first person in her family to go to college. (She tells people that she is a "former" first-generation college student, since her mom went back to school to earn her degree.) She worked her way through school and earned a law degree from Cornell. She was exposed to the highest office in the land when she was a White House Fellow, a program designed for high-achieving people to get a better sense of how government works, under President Barack Obama. Her experience living on Native American reservations, land managed by Native

FUN FACT

Sharice Davids's background as a lawyer is not unusual for a member of Congress, but her years working as a professional mixed martial arts fighter certainly is!

Congresswoman Sharice Davids

American nations, gave her insight into the needs of her community. According to a study conducted by the American Community Survey, one in three Native Americans lives in poverty, and Davids is especially interested in reducing unemployment on reservations.

When she ran in 2018, Davids beat a four-term Republican. She won reelection in 2020. She used her personal experiences in office, but she knows that she cannot speak for every Native American or every gay American. "I would never say that I speak for all Native people or even my tribe," she told the *Advocate* in 2021. "Like any group, Native people are not a monolith. I think it's helpful to constantly remind people of that and make sure that folks know that I might be an expert on my lived experience or certain parts of legislation or policy."

In addition to her identity, she is focused on making life easier for working-class people. "I've been very, very focused on lowering costs. My mom raised me and my brothers by herself. I grew up seeing what it looks like to have to navigate a really tight budget."

Davids is a strong example of a lawmaker who reflects on her life experiences when she considers which policies she wants to fight for in Congress.

THE FIRST OPENLY BISEXUAL PERSON TO SERVE IN CONGRESS

Kyrsten Sinema was born in Tucson, Arizona, in 1976. Her family was middle-class, but her mom and stepdad had money trouble. They divorced, and for a three-year period between the ages of eight and eleven, Kyrsten lived with her mother and siblings in an abandoned Florida gas station with no power and no bathroom. They relied on the local church for food and other necessities. Finally, with the help of the Mormon Church, in 1987, they were able to move into a home. These experiences led Sinema into social work before she got a PhD, a law license, and then threw herself into politics. "I was homeless when I was a kid," she said during her campaign for the House. "But I got my shot at college, I got a job, and I stand before you today."

She started taking classes at a junior college when she was fourteen years old. "Kyrsten was able to open the door for herself, as well as many other students coming after her," said her guidance counselor at the time. "She was just a little adult in teenager's clothing."

In her interview with the *Republic*, Sinema said: "They

told me that I couldn't do it. And I was like, 'Oh no, we're going to do it.' Because I knew that college led to a job and independence."

At thirty-six years old, Kyrsten Sinema became the first openly bisexual member of Congress when she was elected to the House of Representatives in 2012. She joined a record number of LGBTQIA+ candidates who led to a so-called rainbow wave in 2018. Her life story is one of perseverance.

Like so many other firsts, Sinema did not want to dwell on her identity; during her campaigns she rarely mentioned it. After her election in 2012, ABC News asked her what it felt like to be the first openly bisexual member of Congress, and she replied, "We've made history, and we're proud of that, but what I am interested in is making history by making things better for the people of Arizona's Ninth Congressional District." She said that she wanted to use her own family's

"struggle of making it to the middle class" as her guiding light. "I am so honored that Arizonans chose our vision of a better Arizona," she said after she won the 2018 election. "And now it's time to get to work."

Sinema considers the late senator John McCain, who

Representative Kyrsten Sinema speaking with AIPAC

was a famous maverick from Arizona who did things his own way, her hero. Voters in Arizona appreciate politicians who are not partisan: 35 percent identify as Republican, 32 percent Democratic, and 33 percent "other." She started her career as a liberal antiwar state party lawmaker, but since winning her seat in the House in 2012, she has often compromised with Republicans. What the *New York Times* called her "stubborn centrism" has upset Democratic critics who think she sides with Republicans too often. But Sinema sees the need for compromise. In addition to the history-making that she and her colleagues have done by being firsts, most of them want to be known for their legislative accomplishments above their personal stories.

In March 2024, Sinema announced that she would be leaving the Senate when her term was over later that year.

FUN FACT

Sinema is an Ironman triathlete and is decades younger than most of her Senate colleagues.

★ ★ ★

The Ghosts of the Capitol

More than eleven thousand Americans have served as lawmakers, and there have been tens of thousands of staff who have worked in the Capitol. With all those people—and all that history—comes a multitude of ghost stories. Young staffers leaving the office late at night and distracted senators walking down quiet hallways sometimes realize they may not be alone. It is then that they come face-to-face with the past. Here are their stories.

WHO HAUNTS THESE HALLOWED HALLS?

From its very earliest days, when it was still under construction, the Capitol had an eerie quality to it. The building was supposed to be finished by 1800, but because of a series of setbacks, it was not until 1826 that the Rotunda and the Portico were complete.

A professional architect named Benjamin Latrobe steered the ambitious Capitol project forward. Because Washington, D.C., is so hot and humid in the summer, it was decided that the House and Senate Chambers should be moved to the second floor for better air circulation. The new space created on the ground floor would eventually become the Old Supreme Court Chamber. Latrobe hired his friend John Lenthall to supervise construction, but in 1808, when Lenthall decided to remove wooden supports that held up the vaulted ceiling of the Old Supreme Court Chamber, the ceiling collapsed and killed him. According to the author of *Capitol Hill Haunts*, "as he lay dying, [Lenthall] uttered a curse on the building that killed him."

DC, AKA DEMON CAT

There is a ghost so famous on Capitol Hill that it has its own nickname: DC, short for Demon Cat. The first time the enormous creature was seen was in 1862, during the Civil War. Union soldiers defending Washington, D.C., used the Capitol as their dormitory, and stories started circulating about an unusual tabby cat. According to a *Washington Post* story, the cat "fixes its spectral eyes on its hapless victim, with a glow described as 'having all the hue and ferocity of a fire engine entering one of Washington's notoriously dark alleys.'" The victim is stunned into a motionless trance. "This demon cat emits a fierce yowl and with eyes ablaze and mouth open leaps toward the spectator, but invariably leaps quite over his head." The cat then races off and hides in the shadows, waiting to scare another unsuspecting soldier, or later, members of Congress and security guards.

There was so much talk and superstition that one guard even shot at a strange shape, thinking it was the cat. "When I shot at the critter it jumped right over my head." More than thirty-five years passed when no one spotted the cat until, in early October 1898, the *Washington Post* ran a story announcing that the "demon cat" was back.

A sighting of the cat is thought to be a sign of bad news. For instance, the cat was spotted before Abraham Lincoln's assassination in 1865, just before the stock market crash of 1929, and right before John F. Kennedy's assassination in 1963. So its return is never a good sign. But there is a logical reason for the apparition. It was true that there were cats all over the Capitol. There was a rat problem on the Hill, and cats were kept to help lower the population, but after some time, the rats became less of a problem and the cats had nowhere to go. Cats roamed the halls late at night when only security guards and a few members of Congress were around. In 1892, a guard said, "At about ten o'clock every night [groups of cats] begin a mad racing through the empty corridors." The sound of the cats reverberated off the marble floors and stone walls. "The acoustic effects produced are astonishing," according to one newspaper. It would have been frightening to hear the sound of hissing cats in those dark and empty hallways.

Some of the stray cats were adopted by lawmakers, while others wandered into the neighborhood of row houses around the Capitol. The Demon Cat, however, has stayed behind. Some claim that the cat lives in the storage area in the Capitol basement. The area was supposed to be George Washington's tomb; in his will, he made it clear that he wanted to be buried at his beloved Mount Vernon farm instead. The large underground spaces with wide echoing hallways are not ideal places to be alone late at night.

Of course, there is no direct evidence that the Demon Cat exists, but there are tiny paw prints in the floor of the Senate Rotunda that some people swear is proof that it does. In 1898, there was a gas explosion in the Capitol, and in some places new concrete was put down to replace damaged stone. "It's quite possible that a cat walked across the wet concrete," noted Steve Livengood, the chief tour guide of the U.S. Capitol Historical Society. "Just enough to leave some impressions. It's as you come out of the Old Supreme Court Chamber. There may be six or eight pretty clear ones." According to Livengood, the letters "DC" have been etched into the concrete in another part of the building. "Everyone says, 'That's the Demon Cat putting its initials there!'"

THE LIBRARIAN

The Library of Congress opened in 1897 in the ornate Thomas Jefferson Building designed to resemble the Paris opera house. It is the largest library in the world, with millions of books, photographs, newspapers, and recordings.

Before then, the collection was kept in a cramped room in the Capitol. The library was only started in 1800, when President John Adams approved legislation for a small amount of money to buy reference books for members of Congress to use. Washington, D.C., Adams realized, had no libraries because the city was founded only ten years before, in 1790. Like any great European capital, Washington would need to be seen as an intellectual hub, and creating the country's most prestigious library was crucial to that goal.

Before the Thomas Jefferson Building was completed in 1897, a lonely librarian worked in the library. The story goes that he spent years stashing cash inside the pages of the thousands of books he watched over. He never married and did not have children, and sadly passed away before he could collect the large sum of money he had spent years hiding. Because he could never enjoy his money while he was alive, he is said to have stayed, his tortured soul haunting the room in the Capitol where the library was once housed, searching for his money. According to an 1898 account, he was seen wandering around, searching old library shelves for his cash.

Workers reportedly discovered $6,000—an especially large sum of money in the late nineteenth century—when the library relocated to the Jefferson Building.

No one knows for sure who this restless spirit is, but an 1896 *Washington Post* obituary about a long-serving congressional librarian named Charles W. Hoffman is one possibility.

Charles Hoffman, librarian of the Law Library of Congress, 1870s

A trained lawyer, he also worked as dean of the Georgetown Law School and was the law school's first librarian. He might not have ever recovered the $6,000 he hid in the library stacks, but he managed to keep hold of some money. He left behind more than $80,000, which is the equivalent to more than $2,000,000 in today's dollars.

THE BLOODY STEPS

In 1887, Democrat William Preston Taulbee's career was ruined when journalist Charles Kincaid, a Washington correspondent for Taulbee's hometown paper the *Louisville Times*, wrote a scandalous story about his personal life. After he left office, Taulbee became a lobbyist and was a frequent visitor to the Hill. He was a foot taller than Kincaid, and he seemed to enjoy picking on him, sometimes even tugging on his ear. On February 28, 1890, the two men met on the steps outside the House gallery. When Taulbee teased him, Kincaid said that he was "in no condition for a physical contest with you—I am not armed." Taulbee replied, "Then you had better be." Kincaid left and returned hours later. He found Taulbee walking down the stairs on his way to lunch with a friend in the House dining room. Kincaid reportedly said, "Can you see me now?" Then he shot Taulbee. When a policeman rushed to the scene, Kincaid confessed. Taulbee passed away eleven days later, leaving behind his wife and five children. Kincaid was charged with murder, but he was acquitted on the grounds of self-defense.

It is reported that Taulbee's ghost still roams the halls. Sometimes, it is said, he likes to trip reporters as they're coming to work. Taulbee's blood has left a permanent stain on the marble steps so that visitors walking down the steps from the House gallery on the east side of the Capitol can walk on the drops of blood, which are now a deep brown color.

CIVIL WAR SOLDIERS

The Civil War began when shots were fired at Fort Sumter in South Carolina on April 12, 1861. The war led to the deaths of 620,000 Americans and freed nearly four million enslaved people. Within days, soldiers from Union states started coming to Washington, D.C. And the best—and biggest—place to put them was the Capitol.

The Capitol was undergoing construction when the Civil War broke out, but construction stopped abruptly. The first men to arrive were a group of volunteers from Pennsylvania, who stayed in the House of Representatives wing. Then came soldiers from Massachusetts. "The Sixth Regiment of Massachusetts, nine hundred strong, under the command of Col. Jones, were attacked in Baltimore on their way to Washington," said Senate doorkeeper Isaac Bassett. "On arriving here these were marched into the Capitol and immediately occupied the Senate Chamber. . . . The col. made the Vice President's Room his headquarters." The war was devastating, but it was important to give the soldiers basic necessities. A bakery was installed in the basement of the Capitol to make it easy to feed them.

Two weeks after the war began, there were many troops living in the Capitol. Soon the stuffy building started smelling terrible with so many people crammed together. Things only got worse when, in 1862, it was converted into a military hospital. At times, there were a thousand men being treated.

WHO WAS CLARA BARTON?

Clarissa "Clara" Harlowe Barton was born in Massachusetts on Christmas Day in 1821. During the Civil War, she traveled to battlefields and brought supplies to wounded soldiers, earning her the nickname Angel of the Battlefield. She helped reunite more than twenty thousand soldiers with their families. By 1881, when she was fifty-nine years old, she founded the American Red Cross to provide help during humanitarian crises around the country and the world. She served as the Red Cross president until 1904, when she retired. She passed away when she was ninety years old. She lived by this simple motto: "You must never think of anything except the need, and how to meet it."

Clara Barton

The plan to use the Capitol as a hospital was short-lived. Within a year, the wounded soldiers were moved elsewhere so that Congress could meet and because conditions had gotten so bad. Well, all but one soldier left. . . .

In 1898, the *Philadelphia Press* described the soldier who stayed behind: "One of the most curious and alarming of the audible phenomena observable in the Capitol, so all the watchmen say, is a ghostly footstep that seems to follow anybody who crosses Statuary Hall at night."

Many of the wounded soldiers had been treated in Statuary Hall. On July 8, 1906, the *Washington Post* published an account of a Capitol watchman who said he saw a ghost there: "I had been to a part of the building where my duty takes me, and was returning to the western entrance. Just outside Statuary Hall there is an iron staircase, and this I turned to descend. A flash of lighting through a window looking upon the stair lighted up the latter for a second, and in that brief time I caught a glimpse of a figure descending in front of me. I thought it must be one of the other watchmen. The view I caught of the person was not distinct, for whoever it was was at the bottom of the steps while I was at the top. The person kept on ahead of me, though what struck me as peculiar was that I could hear no sound of footsteps. The figure kept on ahead of me at about the same distance as when I first saw it, even though I walked considerably faster in order to come up to it. It descended a certain staircase, and when it reached the bottom and I should say—for, owing to the intense darkness just there I could not see it—there was the loud report of a pistol, and, as I fancied, a cry or groan. I went down, expecting to come upon the scene of a tragedy of some sort, but there were no traces of anything of the sort, and no view of anybody at all."

More than a hundred years after the end of the Civil War, in the 1970s, a Capitol staffer said they heard moaning in Statuary Hall. The person tried to investigate exactly where the sound was coming from, and they said that they traced it to a man wearing a navy-blue military uniform walking across the room. When they got closer, the person was gone. From time to time, people still report seeing the soldier and hearing his moans in the cavernous hall where more than a thousand cots were once placed.

THE GHOST OF JOHN QUINCY ADAMS

On February 21, 1848, John Quincy Adams, who was then eighty years old, suffered a stroke on the floor of the House while he was objecting to the awarding of medals to the generals in the Mexican-American War. (He thought the war was wrong in the first place.) As he rose from his seat to object to ending the debate, he suffered a massive cerebral hemorrhage and was carried to the Rotunda by his colleagues for fresh air and then to the Speaker's Room, where he died two days later. His final words: "This is the last of the earth. I am content." He was buried alongside his wife, his father, and his mother—second president and first lady John and Abigail Adams—at First Parish Church in his family's hometown of Quincy, Massachusetts.

Since his death, the former president has been spotted many times in the Capitol—the place he loved so much. People describe seeing him standing at his desk, attempting to finish his speech. Some even say they can hear him shouting "No!" deep in the night. Others say they can hear his footsteps. The Speaker's Room, where Adams died, was turned into the Lindy Claiborne Boggs Congressional Women's Reading Room, the first room in the Capitol named after a woman. Boggs, a former congresswoman with a wicked sense of humor, said on its dedication in 1991: "When they finally gave us a room, wouldn't you know that they'd give us one that was haunted?"

THE BATHTUBS

One of the strangest—and most delightful—things about the Capitol is its hidden spaces. There are places in this building that not even senators who have been in office for decades know about. And one of the least known aspects of the Capitol is that it once functioned as a sort of spa.

One of the sunken Italian marble bathtubs

In the mid-nineteenth century, when most senators lived nearby in boardinghouses without running water, it was decided that they deserved the chance to take a warm bath in the basement of the Capitol. There was even a masseuse who gave them massages and a barber on-site who cut their hair and trimmed their beards.

In 1859, six large sunken Italian marble bathtubs—three for the Senate and three for the House—were installed and were a popular place to rest and even prepare for floor speeches. Of course, this is when women were not represented in Congress, so the bathtubs were just a place for men. Bright blue and gold tiles were a beautiful contrast to the white tubs.

The Capitol was one of the first places to get running water, so members of Congress could rely on the bathtubs.

In 1888, the *Evening Star* reported that "some of the older members [took] a bath as the last step in their preparation for making a speech. They write the speech, commit it to memory, take a bath and then deliver it." The *Washington Post* described the elegant tubs: "The man proceeds along the warm marble floor to the gigantic basin called a bathtub. It is a solid block of whitest marble, voluptuously curved into a bath, and fitted with gleaming silver faucets, through which gushes filtered hot or cold water. The attendant looks after the water supply, produces a fresh cake of expensive soap for the bather . . . the scent of attar of roses, and the soft delight of fluffy blankets and towels on a downy couch lull him to sleep. He is never disturbed."

Death of the late vice president Henry Wilson in the Vice President's Room at the Capitol

By the 1890s, running water was much more commonplace, and these strange bathtubs became less useful. As a result, four tubs were removed, and the last two tubs were forgotten about. The tubs were discovered during a 1936 excavation project, and people were shocked by the discovery, calling it the "Senate bathtub mystery." No one knew why the tubs were there until a seventy-one-year-old man named Abraham Lincoln Goodall, who had worked in the Capitol as an aide in the 1880s, told the press about it.

The two tubs are still in what is now a maintenance room, but only one is visible. One bathtub is called the "killer tub" because of what happened in it. In 1875, Ulysses S. Grant's vice president, Henry Wilson, who had been in poor health for quite some time, was enjoying his bath a little too much and actually fell asleep—or suffered a stroke; no one knows for sure. When he woke up, he went to the Vice President's Room, where he later died. Some say Wilson has never left the Capitol.

His muffled coughing can reportedly be heard in the office, which is no longer home to the vice president, and some say they can smell the subtle aroma of soap wafting through the air.

★ ★ ★

PERSPECTIVE:

Five Incredible Days on Capitol Hill

* * *

Important Historical Moments

The Capitol has been the site of important moments throughout history that help provide an understanding of what's happening in our world today, and they offer a valuable perspective. From the day the Capitol was almost completely destroyed in 1814; to the moment when President Franklin D. Roosevelt declared that the United States was entering World War II; to 9/11, when the Capitol was a terrorist target; to January 6, 2021, when the Capitol was overtaken by insurrectionists who wanted to overturn the outcome of the 2020 presidential election. Understanding the past helps us make sense of where we are today. And in the end, the story of the Capitol is a story of resilience.

★ ★ ★

August 24, 1814

For twenty-six hours in the summer of 1814, the newly built Capitol was occupied by a foreign army. It was the weather in the city that day that might have saved the building from complete ruin though.

Not many people know that the War of 1812 was the inspiration behind one of the country's most famous and patriotic songs, "The Star-Spangled Banner," the nation's national anthem. The American Revolution ended with Britain's defeat in 1781 at the Battle of Yorktown, but the United States and Great Britain were once again at war three decades later. This time, the war was rooted in a growing sense of American nationalism and British interference in international trade that hurt the U.S. economy. Congress declared war on Great Britain on June 17, 1812.

The war lasted more than two years. During that time, British troops set the White House and the Capitol on fire on the night of August 24, 1814. What happened inside the White House is best known because of a brave decision made by First Lady Dolley Madison. She stayed behind so that a painting of George Washington, known as Gilbert Stuart's *Lansdowne Portrait*, which was hanging in the dining room, could be saved before British soldiers broke in. In a letter she wrote: "Our kind friend, Mr. Carroll, has come to hasten my departure, and is in a very bad humor with me because I insist on waiting until the large picture of Gen. Washington is secured, and it requires to be unscrewed from the wall. This process was found to be too tedious for these perilous moments; I have ordered the frame to be broken, and the canvass taken out it is done, and the precious portrait placed in the hands of two gentlemen of New York for safe keeping."

There is some debate as to how much Dolley actually did to save the famous painting. Paul Jennings was enslaved by the Madisons and was a valet at the White House. His unique memoir gives insight into what life was like inside the White House and what exactly happened the day the British stormed it. "All she [Dolley Madison] carried off was the silver," he wrote. Jennings credited steward John Sioussat and the gardener Thomas McGrath for saving the famous painting. "When the British did arrive they ate up the very dinner and drank the wines that I had prepared for the President's party."

Even less is known about what happened inside the U.S. Capitol. When British troops set fire to the Capitol—which was home to the House, the Senate, the Supreme Court, and the Library of Congress at the time—they mostly focused on public rooms so that the damage they inflicted was clearly visible. Inside what is now National Statuary Hall, soldiers built a massive bonfire and burned furniture and documents. The heat from the fire was so strong that the glass skylights melted. They also made bonfires in the Supreme Court Chamber and in the Library of Congress, which had thousands of books set aflame. The building was not yet complete, and the center building was not yet built, but the damage was still extensive. It could have been much worse, but because fireproof building materials like sandstone and copper were used, it meant that the building could survive.

In the end, something completely out of anyone's control helped save the building. British troops awoke the next day to weather they were not familiar with in England but that was very common in the new Capitol. It was a hot and muggy day, and temperatures tipped one hundred degrees. As local D.C. residents took cover inside, British soldiers ransacked the city, setting fires as they raced through the silent streets. What they didn't realize was that, aside from the presence of the enemy in their city, another reason that residents were huddled inside was because of the storm clouds they saw gathering in the sky. They knew from experience that, when combined with the heat, it meant that a massive storm was on the way. And they were right! The storm was worse than usual. A tornado took shape in the heart of the city and ripped through the streets on its way to the Capitol, where British troops were stationed. Summer thunderstorms were common, but tornadoes were exceedingly rare in Washington. The rain doused the flames, and the storm may have stopped the British from completely destroying the capital city.

The capital city may have been spared, but British troops were eager to claim Baltimore, which was a valuable seaport. On September 13, 1814, British warships began bombing Fort McHenry, the main protection for the city's harbor. The siege lasted for a day. When Francis Scott Key saw the American flag waving above Fort McHenry the next morning, he reflected, "Then in that hour of deliverance and joyful triumph, my heart spoke." He was so inspired by the American victory that he wrote "The Star-Spangled Banner" to celebrate. A peace treaty ending the War of 1812 was ratified by Congress the following year, in 1815.

After members of Congress saw the extensive damage, some argued that the capital should be moved to Philadelphia. But the majority decision was to stay and rebuild, which offered a powerful message of hope and resilience that became central to the nation's story. The burning of the Capitol served only to strengthen the country's resolve.

★ ★ ★

December 8, 1941

Franklin Delano Roosevelt's "Day of Infamy" speech would awaken the sleeping giant. The "sleeping giant" refers to the United States at a time when most Americans wanted to stay out of World War II and focus on problems at home. This was known as the isolationist movement, which was popular because, in the wake of the Great Depression when many Americans were out of work, and with the extensive loss of life experienced during World War I, Americans were not interested in sacrificing their lives for a war being fought across the Atlantic and Pacific Oceans.

But then, on December 7, 1941, Japan attacked the U.S. Naval Base at Pearl Harbor, Hawaii, in a premeditated strike. The early morning was quiet and peaceful on the island of Oahu. Most of the U.S. Pacific Fleet lay at anchor, and planes were side by side on the tarmac. That stillness was violently shattered beginning at 7:55 a.m., when suddenly two hundred Japanese warplanes came into view in the sky. In an hour and fifteen minutes, 2,403 U.S. personnel, including sixty-eight civilians, were killed, and nineteen U.S. Navy ships, including eight battleships, were destroyed or severely damaged. The country was in shock.

It was 1:47 p.m. in Washington, D.C., which is five hours ahead of Hawaii's time zone, when navy secretary Frank Knox called President Roosevelt to tell him what was happening. Roosevelt was in his study in the White House, and he screamed, "NO!" Just three hours after learning about the shocking attack, the president calmly dictated his request to Congress for a declaration of war. He made edits to the speech throughout the night and next morning, using language to convey a sense of urgency. He changed the line that originally read "a date which will live in world history" to the more passionate "a date which will live in infamy." The country was united in its shock and outrage. Roosevelt understood that if he was ever going to get Americans to join the war effort, it was then.

First Lady Eleanor Roosevelt and their son James went with him to the Capitol, where he was to deliver remarks to a joint session of Congress shortly after noon. Roosevelt was paralyzed from the waist down after being diagnosed with polio when he was thirty-nine years old. He was in his wheelchair when he entered a room near the floor of the House of Representatives. But for his speech, he did not want to be seen in his wheelchair. It was 12:29 p.m. when he was announced in the House Chamber and a voice called out, "The president of the United States!" He stood with the use of his heavy leg braces as the room erupted in applause. He walked slowly with a cane and the help of his son to the Speaker's rostrum, and he delivered his remarks to Congress and to the largest-ever radio audience in history. His speech was less than seven minutes long, but it was incredibly powerful. At 1:32 p.m., less than one hour after he finished his speech, the war resolution was approved by the House and Senate. At 4:10 p.m., Roosevelt signed the resolution in the Oval Office, and the United States had officially entered World War II.

January 20, 1961

The Capitol is where most presidents have been sworn in, and that sacred transfer of power is central to democracy. On April 30, 1789, when George Washington was sworn in as the first president, the tradition of an inaugural address was established. Washington took the oath of office on the balcony of New York City's Federal Hall and then read a speech to members of Congress. His second inauguration took place in Philadelphia on March 4, 1793. It was there that Washington delivered the shortest inaugural address on record before he repeated the oath of office.

The most popular and inspirational inaugural addresses seek to pull the country together after the election. Usually the president tries to convey that he is the leader of all people, and that he does not only represent the Americans who voted for him. For example, the address given by Abraham Lincoln in 1865 was designed to unify the country (and it was delivered less than six weeks before he was assassinated). In it, he laid out his principles for peace after the Civil War. The last sentence of his address is often quoted: "With malice toward none; with charity for all; with firmness in the right, as God gives us to see the right, let us strive on to finish the work we are in; to bind up the nation's wounds; to care for him who shall have borne the battle, and for his widow and his orphan—to do all which may achieve and cherish a just, and lasting peace, among ourselves, and with all nations."

In 1933, Franklin Delano Roosevelt delivered a hopeful message in his first inaugural address. Americans were going through the Great Depression, with many citizens not knowing where they would be getting their next meal. Roosevelt famously said, "The only thing we have to fear is fear itself." He argued for the government to step in and ease the suffering.

In 1981, President Ronald Reagan delivered his first inaugural address during another economic downturn. In it, he made the opposite argument from FDR and said less government intervention was the answer and not more. He added, "Those who say that we are in a time when there are no heroes just don't know where to look."

The most famous inaugural address was delivered from the East Front of the Capitol by President John F. Kennedy on January 20, 1961. Kennedy had won the election against Richard Nixon by one of the smallest popular vote margins in history. He knew he needed to try to win over the people who did not vote for him. Like almost every newly elected president, Kennedy reviewed the most successful inaugural speeches before he wrote and gave his own. Nearly one million people gathered in subfreezing temperatures that day for a chance to see Kennedy who, at forty-three years old, was the youngest president ever elected. It had snowed the night before, but it was a clear, sunny day when a clerk of the U.S. Supreme Court held the large family Bible and Kennedy took the oath of office to become the nation's thirty-fifth president. Presidents want to exude confidence, and Kennedy, even in freezing temperatures, took off his topcoat and delivered a stirring and uplifting speech. Kennedy knew he needed to talk about the threats from the Soviet Union during the Cold War without sounding depressing or taking up too much of people's time. "I don't want people to think I'm a windbag," he told his close adviser and speechwriter Ted Sorensen.

Ultimately, while he did not have the shortest address, it was among the shortest at just 1,355 words. The most famous line from his speech was a call to service: "And so, my fellow Americans: ask not what your country can do for you—ask what you can do for your country." He then continued by speaking to the rest of the world: "My fellow citizens of the world: ask not what America will do for you, but what together we can do for the freedom of man."

After his speech, nearly 75 percent of Americans said they approved of President Kennedy.

DID YOU KNOW?

The president who delivered the shortest inaugural address was George Washington, who did not like public speaking. His second inaugural address delivered in Philadelphia on March 4, 1793, was only 135 words long! William Henry Harrison delivered the longest inaugural address, at 8,445 words. He was sworn in on March 4, 1841—which was a cold and wet day. He stood outside in the rain for hours, and one month later, he died of pneumonia. The second president, John Adams, had the longest sentence delivered in any inaugural address at a whopping 2,308 words long.

* * *

September 11, 2001

The morning of September 11, 2001, there was warm weather and clear skies. The White House Residence staff—from the maids, the butlers, and the florists to the cooks—were setting up for a barbecue with members of Congress on the South Lawn. Maids were cleaning the Queens' Bedroom on the second floor, where George H. W. Bush and Barbara had spent the night before. The former president and his wife left at 7:00 a.m. for an early flight. President George W. Bush was in Florida, visiting an elementary school.

Even with all the activity, Laura Bush seemed alone in the White House on the morning of September 11, 2001. She was getting dressed in silence in the Bushes' second-floor bedroom, rehearsing the statement she was going to make at the Senate Health, Education, Labor, and Pensions Committee that morning. She was nervous about her visit to Capitol Hill, where she would be briefing the committee about an early childhood development conference that she'd organized earlier that summer.

It felt like any other busy day at the White House. But of course, that day was anything but typical.

At 9:28 a.m., shortly after two hijacked jetliners struck the twin towers of the World Trade Center in New York City, and minutes before a third plane crashed into the Pentagon, four extremists took over United Flight 93 out of Newark, New Jersey, as the plane headed west over Cleveland, Ohio. The terrorist pilot made a U-turn and dialed the navigational code for Reagan National Airport into the Boeing 757's flight computer, but there was never a plan to land in Washington. The terrorists were either going to hit the White House or the much easier and larger target of the Capitol. The heroism and bravery of the passengers on Flight 93 saved the lives of countless people. They revolted and charged the cockpit, but sadly the plane crashed in a field near Shanksville, Pennsylvania. In less than twenty minutes, the plane would have reached Washington, D.C. It is the only one of the four planes not to have reached its target. But if it had hit either the White House or the Capitol, it would have hit the most visible symbols of the nation's government. "If either the Capitol or the White

House had been hit, it would have been devastating, not only physically, but also psychologically, to the country," said Tom Kean, a Republican former governor of New Jersey who chaired the 9/11 Commission.

No one knows exactly which target they were planning to hit. The definitive report of that awful day was written by the bipartisan National Commission on Terrorist Attacks Upon the United States, which was published in 2004. It did not reach a conclusion other than that the terrorist pilot's "objective was to crash his airliner into symbols of the American Republic, the Capitol or the White House."

First Lady Laura Bush was one of several administration officials dispatched to deal with the crisis. Six days after 9/11, hundreds of family members of the forty passengers and crew of Flight 93 gathered in the desolate field, where the impact of the crash was still fresh. Her visit to Shanksville was emotional. She had private meetings with family members who wanted to know what she and her husband could do to help them recover from their immense loss. "America is learning the names, but you know the people," she told the audience, many of whom were in tears. "And you are the ones they thought of in the last moments of life. You're the ones they called, and prayed to see again. You are the ones they loved." What she did not say, but what she knew in her heart, was that if it were not for those forty passengers and crew members, she might not have survived that day.

Many White House workers credit the passengers on that plane for saving their lives. Laura Bush would have been in danger in either place, the White House or the Capitol. There was a lot of discussion about where to take the first lady during those confusing hours. The Secret Service eventually decided to move her to their own headquarters, a few blocks away from the White House. She sat for hours in a windowless basement conference room, watching the video of the twin towers falling over and over. Eventually she was reunited with her husband and brought to the Presidential Emergency Operations Center beneath the White House. Vice President Dick Cheney and other top officials had been gathered there since that morning. Built for President Franklin Roosevelt during World War II, the command center is accessible only through a series of unfinished underground hallways with pipes hanging down from the ceiling.

There was so much chaos that day, even members of Congress and the president of the United States were having trouble reaching their loved ones because the phone lines were so busy. It impacted everything, including the incredible people who work as telephone operators who can connect any member of Congress to anyone in the world. On September 11, there was no bell signal to evacuate the Capitol. The police had to knock on doors to tell people to leave. Eventually everyone was told to evacuate, including the Capitol operators. The Capitol operators were told to come back after they evacuated. The Capitol Police had not realized that they were the communications hub for all these members who were scattered everywhere. That terrible day, it was the people on Capitol Hill who stayed behind and risked their lives to make sure that democracy functioned who remain examples of the grit and strength of the human spirit.

★ ★ ★

January 6, 2021

On January 6, 2021, what happened during a joint session of Congress to validate who won the presidential election—a routine formality—changed the nation forever. For Fred Johnson, who manages a large catering operation at the Capitol, that Wednesday morning was no different from any other day. He got up early and fought through Washington traffic to make it to work on time. Johnson oversees thirteen restaurants at the House of Representatives. He is a U.S. Air Force veteran, and little did he know that morning that when the Capitol was under attack, he would use the crisis-management skills he learned in the military and his culinary skills in the kitchen.

Around 8:00 a.m., Johnson checked on the food outlets that were open. He was too busy doing his job to follow what was on cable news that day. He knew the bitter 2020 election was over, and that Joe Biden had defeated Donald Trump, and he knew that members of Congress were in town to formally verify the election results.

It was expected that several Republicans would object to the certification process, but a violent mob breaking into the Capitol was not what most people were expecting that day. When then president Donald Trump spoke to supporters

DID YOU KNOW?

The electoral college is made up of people chosen to represent their state. Each state has a number of electors equal to their number of representatives in the House and the Senate. There are 538 electors, and a majority of 270 is required to elect the president. The founding fathers came up with this system as a compromise; some thought that Congress should elect the president, and some made the case that the president should be elected by popular vote (back then, only white men with property could vote).

The process of verifying the election results involves certifying the state-by-state results of the electoral around noon near the White House, things changed. "We will never give up. We will never concede," Trump told his supporters at the rally. He said the election was fraudulent, and he insisted that he had won, not Joe Biden. He called on his vice president, Mike Pence—as the president of the Senate—to refuse to accept Biden's victory and send the votes back to the states. "Mike Pence, I hope you're going to stand up for the good of our Constitution and for the good

college. Electors meet in their states after the general election, and they cast their votes for president and vice president on separate ballots. Each state's electoral vote is sent to Congress, where the votes are counted in a joint session of Congress on January 6, after the election. Members of the House and Senate gather in the House Chamber to conduct the official count of electoral votes. The vice president, as president of the Senate, presides over the count and announces the results. He or she then declares who has been elected president and vice president of the United States.

of our country," Trump said. "And if you're not, I'm going to be very disappointed in you."

At around 1:00 p.m., Pence released a letter that said he would not follow Trump's orders, and that his role certifying electoral votes was mostly ceremonial anyway. "My oath to support and defend the Constitution constrains me from claiming unilateral authority to determine which electoral votes should be counted and which should not," Pence wrote.

In the meantime, Trump called on his supporters to march toward the Capitol building, though he decided to stay at the White House. "We fight like hell," he said. "And if you don't fight like hell, you're not going to have a country anymore." Crowds had already started gathering at the Capitol, even as Trump was speaking. Inside the Capitol, people were just trying to do their jobs. Shortly after 1:00 p.m., Fred Johnson got a call telling him that one of the buildings was being evacuated, and twenty minutes later, he was watching television in his office and saw people hanging off the front steps of the Capitol. "That's when it started hitting home," he recalled. He instructed the people he supervised to go to the cafeteria in the Longworth office building and shelter there. "When you're working in the kitchen you have no idea what's going on outside." He told employees to grab their coats and keys and to have their badges showing so that security could see that they were supposed to be there.

On the way to the Longworth House Office Building, they saw Capitol Police and flashed their badges to get inside. "One thing I remember," Johnson said, "in the military, as long as you're calm everyone else will be calm." About forty kitchen staff and eight or nine managers stayed in the cafeteria for six hours, watching the violence that was happening so close to them on television.

Outside the walls of the Capitol, the scene was growing more and more chaotic. By 1:30 p.m. protestors had overcome the police. Capitol Police officer Cam Sikurinec remembered the crowd yelling at him: "Are you traitors or are you with [Congress] or with us?" He was standing at the East Front of the Capitol, and he knew things were getting bad at the West Front because of what he was hearing on his walkie-talkie. Members of the mob that had gathered were throwing things and pushing down barricades. "It was chaos from the crowd, it was chaos on the radios. You couldn't hear any police direction from any type of supervising officer on the radio, what to do, where to go. Everything happened so fast."

The crowd raced up the East Plaza steps to the Rotunda door. Sikurinec and four other officers hurried toward the Rotunda. "The first thing I remember seeing was officers sitting on chairs and other officers flushing their eyes out with water. They had already been sprayed by the crowd or blowback spray from other officers." The next thing he heard was someone yelling: "Get down to the crypt! They're breaking down the door!" He ran to the crypt with a few other officers. The crowd was inside already and started running toward them. About fifteen officers stood in the crypt, trying to hold the mob back, locking arms in a chain and standing in a line. There were chairs flying at them and so much shouting they could not hear a thing.

DID YOU KNOW?

What does "insurrectionist" mean? An insurrectionist is a person who takes part in an armed rebellion against an established government.

Audra Jackson came to Washington in 2016, when she graduated from college. By 2019, she was assistant manager at the House Democratic Cloakroom. She was working on the House floor during the insurrection.

She said she was "a little nervous" on January 6 but also excited. She knew the day was an important part of American democracy. To her, it represented the peaceful transfer of power, but once the attack began, she raced to the back of the cloakroom, terrified. "They were beating on the door, and luckily it wasn't one or two minutes before we all evacuated the House Chamber. If it had been any slower, they would have seen us." She went out with members of Congress. The whole time, she was texting her father as he was watching the scene unfold on television. She said she would have been more scared if she saw what her father was seeing. "We didn't know how bad it was."

Jackson was essential to the process of certifying the election, so after three hours in a safe location, she and her colleagues returned to their offices. "We just kept going, and we left around 4:00 a.m. that morning. That was the best decision I made, because if I hadn't gone back to my office I probably never would have come back to the Hill. I would have been too scared."

Emma Kaplan was working that day as the floor adviser to then Speaker of the House Nancy Pelosi. In her role, she worked with parliamentarians and the clerk's office on rules of the House, trying to get legislation passed. She knew January 6 was an important day, and she was a little anxious, but she never expected violence. When Speaker Pelosi was ushered off the House floor shortly after 2:00 p.m., Kaplan knew things were bad. That was around the time the mob broke windows and climbed into the Capitol building.

Members of Congress were told to be seated, and on both sides of the aisle, Republicans and Democrats were helping each other put on emergency gas masks that were kept under their seats. Kaplan helped them too. "I was in staffer mode. If I had stopped to think about it, I would have been worse off." She says she won't forget the sound of those masks with so many people wearing them. "They make this horrific whirring sound, and when you have one hundred of them on in a room as cavernous as the House Chamber, it is loud." She was relieved once she knew that the doors were locked and no one could get in while they were there, but she had no idea where the insurrectionists were. She was eventually taken into a large room in the Longworth House Office Building with other staff and members of Congress.

She and her colleagues were determined not to let the fear and violence of that day stop them from doing their jobs and certifying the election. Once they were told the Capitol was clear, the parliamentarians, the clerk staff, and the floor team were allowed back in. They needed to get documents ready. They went with a security escort back into the chamber while members waited to return. Kaplan remembered the floors being a different color and sticky, and she spotted a poster on the floor left behind by an insurrectionist. It read, *Save the Republic.* It was a crime scene that needed to be investigated, and they spent a little time cleaning up the floor of the chamber to get it ready for the work that brought them there. "My mindset was, 'Let's get to work.' There was never any option but to go on," Kaplan said. She went home between four and five the next morning.

Jordan Wilson was an aide to a Republican member of Congress when he had the opportunity to work for the inaugural committee, a joint congressional committee that prepares for the inauguration. Even though Wilson was a Republican and the new president, Joe Biden, was a Democrat, Wilson was proud to be part of this tradition. Speaker Nancy Pelosi, a Democrat, served on the committee with Congressman Kevin McCarthy, House Republican leader. It was Wilson's fourth day working on the inauguration when someone ran into the room and yelled, "They're almost to the Capitol!" It wasn't even on TV yet at that point, so he and his colleagues started checking social media. The Capitol was put on lockdown and they sheltered in place. They moved bookcases and desks in front of doors, and one of their first thoughts was to lock books about inaugurations they were using for research in drawers so that they could not be taken or destroyed. About a dozen people remained barricaded in the room for several hours.

Eventually police escorted Wilson and his colleagues out through the crypt. As he walked through, Wilson could not believe what he was seeing. "I love this place," he said. "Since middle school I wanted to intern on the Hill. That was my big dream. So here I am in this place I have so much reverence for, and the crypt is always quiet because people respect the space and it's just so much history [there]. The lights were very dim so it looked eerie and there was water all over the floor and they had started to tear gas the crowd and there were fifteen or twenty Capitol Police officers that had been tear-gassed that were just yelling on the floor because they couldn't see . . . one person spit when I walked by. It was just the polar opposite of the space that I know."

Once it was announced that lawmakers and staff were going to continue their work and certify the election, Wilson and his colleagues were escorted back to work. After January 6, he said, they were even more driven. "I had this mission of putting on the inauguration. . . . It gives me goose bumps when I think about this, the theme of the inauguration was

'Our Determined Democracy.' And that was decided months before any of this happened . . . and so we just kept saying, 'We're determined.' . . . They wheeled cots next to our desks and we'd work until 3:00 a.m., sleep a couple hours, wake back up at five, and do it all over again. We didn't have time."

For law enforcement, there was no relief that day. Capitol Police officer Sikurinec remembered going to the Cannon House Office Building. He was told to keep a tunnel clear as an evacuation spot. Officers were walking into the tunnel with their eyes burning from tear gas. Congressional staffers walking through the tunnel looked stunned. "You could see the fright in their eyes, and they could probably see the fright in ours. Because this whole thing was just scary."

He went to the Longworth House Office Building, where members of Congress and staff were trying to leave and needed an officer to provide them safe passage. Later in the evening, he gathered with other officers to determine who was hurt and who needed to go to the hospital. The fire department came to help people who had been tear-gassed. Because Congress was back in session and they would be certifying votes until early the next morning, Sikurinec knew that he and his fellow officers would have to stay and work in rotations.

At 4:00 a.m. he went to sleep in his car, then went back at 9:00 a.m. The pace continued for a while; they were on sixteen-hour shifts and then twelve-hour shifts for a couple of weeks,

Senator Bob Menendez presents a flag to Brian Sicknick's family.

with limited days off. But they would do anything to make sure that something like January 6 never happened again.

Officer Sikurinec has a simple message for the people who forced their way into the Capitol: "Don't turn your First Amendment right into a criminal act."

At the end of the day, Fred Johnson's dining staff was exhausted, but he made the case that it was the right thing to do to stay and feed people who were traumatized and in need of a decent meal. "When the world is falling apart you realize how important creature comforts are. It was unorthodox, but we heated up the grill and fed them pizza, burgers, french fries, and chicken tenders, and it brought people a sense of relief." Johnson and five managers stayed until midnight, and he estimated that they fed more than five hundred people, including police officers, staff, and members of Congress.

Several people lost their lives because of what happened on January 6, including U.S. Capitol Police officer Brian Sicknick and Trump supporter Ashli Babbitt. But even those who were not harmed physically lost something that day: they lost the sense of comfort they once had at work. Now people are trying to rebuild that sense of community so important to the people who work at the Capitol.

After the siege, the staff was left to clean up the mess. Members of Congress helped too. Congressman Andy King, a Democrat from New Jersey and the first Asian American ever to represent New Jersey in Congress, was seen in a photograph that went viral, on his hands and knees in the Rotunda, cleaning up water bottles, pieces of body armor, and destroyed pieces of furniture. "It's a room that I love so much—it's the heart of the Capitol, literally the heart of this country," King said. "It pained me so much to see it in this kind of condition." He worked for an hour and a half filling trash bags. He did not stop there; afterward he went to National Statuary Hall and the Capitol crypt.

King was profoundly impacted by the events of January 6. "I feel blessed to have this opportunity as a son of immigrants to be able to serve in Congress," he said. "Democracy to me is this place of opportunity that is affording me a chance to do something extraordinary."

For weeks after the attack, the Capitol was under the tightest security imaginable. Concrete barricades and black metal fences too tall to climb lined the perimeter, and armed police officers were stationed everywhere. More than six thousand members of the National Guard from six states— Virginia, Pennsylvania, New York, New Jersey, Delaware, and Maryland—were brought in to help the Capitol Police and other law enforcement for weeks afterward.

Audra Jackson, the young woman who worked in the Democratic Cloakroom, felt "like there should be some level of accountability for what happened . . . to know all the lives that these people affected. My life is different . . . I saw how resilient I am . . . the dark days, the anxious moments I got through. . . . My job is still a part of history each and every day, working on the House floor."

For Emma Kaplan in Speaker Nancy Pelosi's office, what happened on January 6 did not make her want to leave her job. Instead, she said, "It felt like a reason to stay."

★ ★ ★

Epilogue

Washington, D.C., is a hub for ambitious and curious people, many of whom want to devote their lives to building upon the progress of the last 250 years. They want to soak up the history of the Capitol building, where presidents have been sworn into office and where, after their deaths, they lie in state in the Capitol Rotunda.

From the first cornerstone laid by President George Washington, the Capitol has represented freedom and democracy. But part of the evolution of the Capitol is the influx of people who have come from all over the country to work there, from subway operators and painters to legislative aides and chiefs of staff. They come from all walks of life and bring their unique life experiences with them. Office staff come to Washington and work twelve-hour days at pay far less than in the private sector. They can be asked to do anything from driving their boss (a member of Congress) to a meeting to helping to draft an important bill.

We know about the remarkable people who made history when they became the first person with their background to be elected to Congress, whether that's because of their race, gender, heritage, or sexual identity. But the stories you don't hear about are from people like Christine McCreary, who worked on Capitol Hill for forty-five years and who was one of the first Black staffers to challenge de facto segregation on the Hill.

When McCreary moved to Washington in 1953, the city was still segregated, and there were hardly any Black people working for members of Congress. McCreary was one of the first people to question this injustice. McCreary saw the staff sizes of senators get bigger and bigger. When she started her career, the entire Senate staff worked out of one Senate office building. When she retired, there were three office buildings for staff. She worked all over the Hill, from the Old Senate Office Building (later named the Richard Russell Building) with its chandeliers and floor-to-ceiling mahogany doors to the newest building (named for Senator Philip A. Hart), which is much more modern. Not only did she see more diversity among her colleagues, she also saw more people of color on the Senate floor. McCreary passed away in 2006.

Bertie Bowman

Herbert "Bertie" Bowman arrived in Washington a decade before McCreary and spent more than sixty years working on Capitol Hill. He was the longest-serving Black congressional staffer in history, and when he died in 2023, tributes came pouring in from Democrats and Republicans, including one from President Bill Clinton. Bowman came from modest roots and arrived in Washington in 1944, a decade before the civil rights movement began. His first job was sweeping the Capitol steps, and eventually he was hired as a clerk on the powerful Senate Committee on Foreign Relations, where he stayed until he was ninety years old. "This," he said, "is the American dream."

The people who work behind the scenes at the Capitol have left their marks on members of Congress too. The changes we can see are sometimes just as important as the changes that happen behind closed doors.

A white marble compass stone lies on the sandstone floor of the Capitol crypt, which was meant to be George Washington's final resting place. The circular room is surrounded by forty tall columns. The compass stone marks the very center of the Capitol building and the middle of the capital city. It radiates out like a sunburst dividing Washington into four quadrants: northeast, northwest, southeast, and southwest. Pierre L'Enfant designed the city so that numbered streets run north to south and lettered streets go east to west. Diagonal avenues are named after states. The city's symmetry, and the compass stone itself, are symbols of unity. The stone's marble, worn by years of people walking on it, reminds visitors that no matter how divided the country

View of the star in the center of the crypt floor

272

is, there are central tenets Americans hold dear. Democracy has its own moral compass.

Members of Congress were so determined to transfer George Washington's remains from his Mount Vernon home to the Capitol tomb, even years after his burial, because they understood how important symbolism has always been to the country. The Capitol embodies democracy. Unlike the White House, which serves a dual function as a private home for the president and his family, the Capitol truly belongs to everyone.

The tomb intended for George and Martha Washington is located beneath the compass stone, and it sits empty still. But there were members of Congress who would not let it go. After Washington's death in 1799, Congress sent a letter to Martha Washington asking for her approval, which she granted reluctantly: "Taught by the great example which I have so long had before me never to oppose my private wishes to the public will, I need not, I cannot, say what a sacrifice of individual feeling I make to a sense of public duty."

The country's very first first lady knew that her husband, as the first president, represented the fight for independence and the birth of the country. But the first attempt to remove his remains failed because Washington stated in his will that he wanted to be buried at his Mount Vernon estate in northern Virginia. Not everyone took Washington's will as the final verdict. In President John Quincy Adams's first annual message to Congress on December 6, 1825, more than twenty-five years after Washington's death, he asked members to complete unfinished business: "A spot has been reserved within the walls where you are deliberating for the benefit of this and future ages in which the mortal remains may be deposited of him whose spirit hovers over you and listens with delight to every act of the representatives of this nation which can tend to exalt and adorn his and their country." According to Adams, it was their patriotic duty to move the remains to the Capitol, which was to be completed in 1826. But years passed and nothing happened. In 1832, the centennial of Washington's birth, the movement was revived yet again. Virginia lawmakers opposed the idea, and Congress could not get the consent of all of Martha Washington's relatives, one of whom cited Washington's stated desire to be buried at Mount Vernon.

Moving Washington's remains to the Capitol shows how much the young country relied on symbolism to remind the world of its unique place in history. There is no other country like the United States, and no other place like the Capitol, with its constant rotation of new voices and new statues honoring the voices of the past. The Capitol dome is a symbol of American resilience and tolerance for growth and change. Like the country, the Capitol building is a work in progress, ever evolving.

It makes sense that there was a decades-long debate about transferring Washington's remains; he is the embodiment of the country's fight for independence and its bold rebellious spirit. But Washington's wish to be buried at his home is proof that he believed in the enduring strength of democracy. While symbols, like the compass stone, are important, it's the ideas behind them that matter most.

★ ★ ★

Acknowledgments

My conversations for this book began in a coffee shop in Washington, D.C., where I met Donald Ritchie, the Senate historian emeritus. "We're there to provide a service, which was instilled in me in the military," he told me. "I don't do politics." He had recently retired and was eager to point me in the direction of the best sources for information about the Capitol. I am grateful to him for his time and to his unwavering dedication to preserving American history.

Fred Johnson and John Bean are colleagues and also good friends. They gave me a tour of the shops in the basement of the Capitol, and they took the time to introduce me to their colleagues, many of whom they had known for years. Emmanuel Bolden shared beautiful stories of working with his father, Alvin, who passed away in 2022. Alvin taught his son his craft as a shoe shiner working steps away from the Capitol subway. I may have interrupted Tim Magruder, the supervisor in the Finishing Shop, while he was sanding down a wood frame heading to a member of Congress's office, but he did not make me feel like it. He was very open and honest. Mary Baumann and Kate Scott, who work in the Senate Historical Office, provided eye-opening material, as did Gian Panetta, who shared wonderful stories of his grandmother Tina. I owe Kathryn Lyons a debt of gratitude for putting me in touch with Gian. Chip Unruh, a Capitol Hill veteran, generously connected me with his colleagues.

Finally, I'd like to offer special thanks to Yianni Varonis at the U.S. Capitol Historical Society, who has put together a fascinating January 6 Oral History Project. Hearing the words of Emma Kaplan, Cam Sikurinec, Audra Jackson, and Jordan Wilson, some of the people who were working inside the Capitol that day, provides a much deeper understanding of the fear they felt and brings a sense of urgency to the story that I hope remains for hundreds of years.

Selected Bibliography

Alexander, John. *Ghosts: Washington Revisited*. Atglen, PA: Schiffer, 1998.

Charles River Editors. *Building America's Main Seats of Power: The Construction History of the White House and U.S. Capitol*. Charles River Editors, 2015.

———. *The United States Capitol Building: The History and Legacy of the Seat of Congress*. Charles River Editors, 2015.

Jennings, Paul. *A Colored Man's Reminiscences of James Madison*. Brooklyn, NY: G. C. Beadle, 1865.

MacNeil, Neil, and Richard A. Baker. *The American Senate: An Insider's History*. Oxford; New York: Oxford University Press, 2013.

Miller, William "Fishbait," with Frances Spatz Leighton. *Fishbait: The Memoirs of the Congressional Doorkeeper*. Englewood Cliffs, NJ: Prentice-Hall, 1977.

Moser, Edward P. *The Lost History of the Capitol: The Hidden and Tumultuous Saga of Congress and the Capitol Building*. Guilford, CT: Lyons, 2021.

Parker, Robert, with Richard Rashke. *Capitol Hill in Black and White*. New York: Dodd, Mead & Company, 1986.

Remini, Robert V. *The House: The History of the House of Representatives*. New York: HarperCollins, 2006.

★ ★ ★

Recommended Reading

Brower, Kate Andersen. *Exploring the White House: Inside America's Most Famous Home.* New York: HarperCollins, 2020.

Flynn, Sarah Wassner. *1,000 Facts about the White House.* Washington, D.C.: National Geographic, 2017.

Grove, Noel. *Inside the White House: Stories from the World's Most Famous Residence.* Washington, D.C.: National Geographic, 2013.

House, Katherine L. *The White House for Kids: A History of a Home, Office, and National Symbol.* Chicago: Chicago Review Press, 2014.

Monkman, Betty C. *The White House: Its Historic Furnishings and First Families.* Washington, D.C.: White House Historical Association, 2000.

Reis, Ronald A. *The US Congress for Kids: Over 200 Years of Lawmaking, Deal-Breaking, and Compromising.* Chicago: Chicago Review Press, 2014.

Stine, Megan. *Where Is the White House?* New York: Penguin, 2015.

* * *

Chapter Notes

PLACES

"As good government . . . to a few of the most wise and good.": John Adams, "Thoughts on Government," April 1776, United States Senate, Primary Documents, www.senate.gov/artandhistory/history/common/generic/exerpt-thoughts-on-government-adams-1776.htm.

"I walk on untrodden ground": The Mount Vernon Ladies' Association, "10 Facts about President Washington's Election," www.mountvernon.org/george-washington/the-first-president/election/10-facts-about-washingtons-election.

"music playing, drums beating, colors flying, and spectators rejoicing.": Architect of the Capitol, "First Cornerstone," www.aoc.gov/explore-capitol-campus/art/first-cornerstone.

"a pedestal waiting for a monument.": Andrew Glass, "Washington Lays Capitol Cornerstone, September 18, 1793," *Politico*, September 18, 2014.

"I have seen [slaves] in large numbers . . . What a country of liberty.": Sarah Fling, "Enslaved Labor and the Construction of the U.S. Capitol," The White House Historical Association, www.whitehousehistory.org/enslaved-labor-and-the-construction-of-the-u-s-capitol.

"Married on Capitol Dome: Young Couple Made Man and Wife 375 Feet Above Ground at Washington.": *New York Times*, March 27, 1902.

"the very center of the Free World.": Ira R. Allen, "Emigre to Moscow Bride: 'I love you,'" United Press International, UPI Archives, May 10, 1982.

"It's very sweet and very romantic.": *Buffalo News* Staff, "Capitol Plans," *Buffalo News*, February 9, 1996.

"shall from time to time . . . necessary and expedient.": U.S. Const. art. II, § 3.

"Emancipate, Enfranchise, [and to] Educate": Henry Highland Garnet, "Let the Monster Perish," February 12, 1865, BlackPast.org, www.blackpast.org/african-american-history/1865-henry-highland-garnet-let-monster-perish/.

"Upon the total and complete destruction of this accursed sin depends the safety and perpetuity of our Republic and its excellent institutions.": Ibid.

"Every member shall remain uncovered during the sessions of the House.": U.S. House of Representatives, History, Art & Archives, "The Ban on Hats on

281

the House Floor," history.house.gov/Historical-Highlights/1800-1850/The
-debate-over-the-rule-to-ban-hats-on-the-House-Floor/.

"the taking of pictures of any kind": U.S. Senate, "Smile: Photographing the
Senate in Session," www.senate.gov/about/historic-buildings-spaces
/chamber/photographing-senate-in-session.htm.

"The fact . . . know they will be called to terrible account.": Senate Historical Office,
"Senate Stories: Churchill's Historic Speech to Congress," May 2, 2022,
www.senate.gov/artandhistory/senate-stories/churchills-historic-speech
-to-congress.htm.

"illegal, improper, or unethical activities": U.S. Senate, "Select Committee on
Presidential Campaign Activities," www.senate.gov/about/powers-procedures
/investigations/watergate.htm.

"What did the president know and when did he know it?": Connie Cass,
"Remembering Howard Baker, Whose Famous Question Embodies the
Watergate Hearings," PBS News, June 26, 2014, www.pbs.org/newshour
/politics/remembering-howard-baker-whose-famous-question-embodied
-watergate-hearings.

"Why cannot we stop at hotels here without . . . our white colleagues on this
floor?": Bobby J. Donaldson and Christopher Frear, "Meet Joseph Rainey,
the First Black Congressman," *Smithsonian*, January 2021.

"He was a man of dignity . . . different types of establishments": David Russell,
"Lorna Rainey Honors Trailblazing Family," *Queens Chronicle*, April 4, 2019.

"I always look at this and go . . . you just can't allow them to": Ibid.

"We talked about what it was like . . . She was tired of the injustice.": Ashley
Southall, "Statue of Rosa Parks Is Unveiled at the Capitol," *New York Times*,
February 27, 2013.

"People always say that I didn't give up my seat . . . was tired of giving in.": Rosa
Parks with Jim Haskins, *Rosa Parks: My Story* (New York: Dial Books,
1992), 116.

"My hand is not the color of yours . . . I am a man.": Gillian Brockell, "Civil
Rights Leader 'Almost Nobody Knows About' Gets a Statue in the U.S.
Capitol," *Washington Post*, September 20, 2019.

"an Indian is a 'person' . . . weak, insignificant, unlettered and generally despised
race.": Ibid.

"one of the most important civil rights leaders in our country": Ibid.

"I hope that Sojourner Truth would be proud to see me . . . the face of a woman who
looks like them.": Office of the First Lady, "Remarks by the First Lady at the
Sojourner Truth Bust Unveiling," April 28, 2009, obamawhitehouse.archives
.gov/the-press-office/remarks-first-lady-sojourner-truth-bust-unveiling.

"so tall within, as if the power of a nation was within [her].": The Faith Project, "Sojourner Truth," PBS, www.pbs.org/thisfarbyfaith/people/sojourner_truth .html.

"That man over there says that women need to be helped . . . these women together ought to be able to turn it back, and get it right side up again!": "Sojourner Truth: Ain't I a Woman?", National Parks Service, www.nps.gov /articles/sojourner-truth.htm.

"I, for one, am proud that our country could produce a Mrs. Bethune.": "Mary McLeod Bethune and Eleanor Roosevelt Comment on America's Imperfect Democracy," NYC Municipal Archives WNYC Collection, Annotations: The NEH Preservation Project, New York Public Radio, August 3, 2012.

"I remember as a little girl listening . . . what seemed impossible, possible.": Adam Harris, "The Val Demings Gamble," *Atlantic*, September 6, 2022.

"Is there anything we can do for you? You are the one in trouble now.": Scott Bomboy, "Looking Back at the Day FDR Died," *Constitution Daily* (blog), National Constitution Center, April 12, 2024, constitutioncenter.org/blog /looking-back-at-the-day-fdr-died.

"With these necessary steps, President Truman . . . the prosperity of this great nation.": Daniel Desrochers, "Missouri Icon Harry Truman Strides Back into U.S. Capitol as Long-Awaited Statue Unveiled," *Kansas City Star*, September 30, 2022.

"I leave you today with my family's deep gratitude . . . 'Do your duty and history will do you justice.'": Ibid.

"old wooden phone booths like Superman . . . that goes on to circulate the air.": Martin P. Paone, Oral History Project, U.S. Senate, www.senate.gov/about /oral-history/paone-martin-oral-history.htm.

"people call in, mostly from the offices . . . especially in the days before they were on TV.": Ibid.

"Then you have five page lines, also . . . All that changed with email.": Ibid.

"They'd be out there and you can hear them . . . wanting to know where this was coming from.": Ibid.

"In the olden days, we had Northern water and Southern water . . . Eventually, we just stuck with Poland Springs.": Ibid.

"other senators wanted the Democratic cloakroom to be more . . . without being encumbered by staff.": Ibid.

"little kingdom[s]": Leonard H. Ballard, Oral History Project, U.S. Senate, www .senate.gov/about/oral-history/ballard-leonard-h-oral-history.htm.

"You don't tell any person . . . but you don't tell anybody that, particularly the press.": Ibid.

"I think it is how I got along. I stayed here through . . . Nobody ever bothered with me.": Ibid.

"In my old hideaway we had ghosts . . . it had moved around by itself about every two or three months.": Jordy Yager, "Haunted House—and Senate," *The Hill*, March 3, 2009.

"Your Superfluous Excellency": Valerie Haeder, "His Superfluous Excellency: Tales of the Vice Presidency," *Headlines & Heroes* (blog), Library of Congress, February 18, 2019, blogs.loc.gov/headlinesandheroes/2019/02 /his-superfluous-excellency-tales-of-the-vice-presidency.

"I enjoyed my time as vice president . . . mandatory eleven hours of sleep a day.": Tim Mak, "11 Insults about Being Vice President," *Politico*, August 8, 2012, www.politico.com/gallery/11-insults-about-being-vice-president?slide=4.

"The vice president simply presides over the Senate and sits around hoping for a funeral.": David McCullough, "'I Hardly Know Truman,'" *American Heritage* 43, no. 4 (July/August 1992), www.americanheritage.com/i-hardly -know-truman#.

"I'm so happy to be here, I finally get to be a Senate wife!": Kate Andersen Brower, *First in Line: Presidents, Vice Presidents, and the Pursuit of Power* (New York: Harper, 2018).

"Being cast in marble is something every vice president looks forward to . . . our one shot at being remembered.": Ibid.

PEOPLE

"In the good old days when I was a senator, I was my own man.": Mark Leibovich, "For a Blunt Biden, an Uneasy Supporting Role," *New York Times*, May 7, 2012.

"I find that the prejudice in this country to color is very great, and I sometimes fear that it is on the increase.": Jennifer Latson, "How the First Black U.S. Senator Was Nearly Kept from His Seat," *TIME*, February 25, 2015, time .com/3714088/hiram-revels/.

"Not many people make history for a job . . . Refinishing is my interpretation of what I want a piece of furniture to look like.": Author interview with Tim Magruder.

"a great haircut, but it's more than a haircut": Stefani Dazlo, "House Barber 'Joe Q' Makes Politicians Part of His Family," *Washington Post*, March 14, 2012.

"This is a family barbershop . . . We got a lot of friends who come in, shoot the breeze.": Ibid.

"I came here like a fish out of water, and look where I'm at . . . It's the best job because you come in contact with everybody.": Kristi King, "'The House Barber'

Retires after 52 Years of Capitol Hill Cuts," WTOP News, August 26, 2022.

"I think it's one of the best jobs . . . And I'm a part of it.": Dazlo, "House Barber 'Joe Q' Makes Politicians Part of His Family."

"Every step of the way things have changed . . . People don't speak to each other as much as they used to.": Author interview with Mario D'Angelo.

"David Miles Knight—the beloved barber in our barbershop . . . regale those folks with stories about his family.": Graham Vyse, "The Senate Has Its Own Longstanding, Secretive Basement Barbershop," DCist, June 17, 2019.

"to help senators cope with the dirt and distances of Washington . . . paid the salaries of barbers.": Ibid

"I heard a lot of conversations between senators, but I never talked about it with anyone.": Phil Gailey, "For Senate, a New Era in Grooming," *New York Times*, September 7, 1981.

"wholesome refreshments": Andrew Glass, "House Debates Merits of Club Sandwich, May 6, 1930," *Politico*, May 6, 2018, www.politico.com/story/2018/05/06/house-debates-merits-of-club-sandwich-may-6-1930-570725.

"be served in the House every day, regardless of the weather.": Kathryn Lyons and Katherine Tully-McManus, "First It Was Lawmakers, Now Members' Dining Room Has To Deal with Yelp," *Roll Call*, October 24, 2019, rollcall.com/2019/10/24/first-it-was-lawmakers-now-members-dining-room-has-to-deal-with-yelp/.

"We aren't political people . . . as good as it can be for members.": Author interview with Fred Johnson.

"When you're walking around Capitol Hill with a chef coat you meet a lot of people!": Ibid.

"If I needed a table saw or a vacuum cleaner, I knew who to ask.": Ibid.

"I gave them a couple dozen doughnuts as a thank-you.": Ibid.

"It's like any job . . . you don't talk politics or religion.": Author interview with Robert Remsburg.

"She brought that motherly vibe to the Capitol": Author interview with Gian Panetta.

"She's a simple person in a complex world . . . 'How are the kids?'": Ibid.

"cute" . . . "little suits.": Ibid.

"At a time of polarization, Tina's story reminds us of our common bonds both in Congress and in the country.": Margaret Foster, "Tina Panetta, Mother on the Hill," *Beacon*, February 26, 2021, www.thebeaconnewspapers.com/tina-panetta-mother-on-the-hill/.

"It's been a magical journey . . . the money and reward come naturally.": Author interview with Emmanuel Bolden.

285

"I always met people who knew more than I did.": Ibid.

"He taught me the trade and technique . . . whether it's shining shoes or anything else.": Ibid.

"I did the feet, and he did the hair . . . It was killing two birds with one stone.": Author interview with Alvin Bolden.

"The shoe shop is a place for them to unwind . . . The shoe shining is just the cherry on top.": Author interview with Emmanuel Bolden.

"He has a smile [that] covers his whole face.": Lisa Desjardins, "Subway Driver Outlasts Senators, Retires after 41 Years Below the Capitol," CNN, May 2, 2014, www.cnn.com/2014/05/01/politics/capitol-hill-subway-driver/index.html.

"He's the happiest guy you ever met. He has a genius for lifting people's spirits.": Ibid.

"probably the most unusual subway car ride": Architect of the Capitol, "Capitol Subway System," www.aoc.gov/explore-capitol-campus/buildings-grounds /capitol-building/capitol-subway-system.

"elegant": Ibid.

"The people you meet on the train . . . you meet new people all the time.": Author interview with Dave Anderson.

"As messenger to the Doorkeeper . . . and for every bill that is passed perhaps five hundred fall by the wayside.": William Miller with Frances Spatz Leighton, *Fishbait: The Memoirs of the Congressional Doorkeeper* (Englewood Cliffs, N.J.: Prentice-Hall, c. 1977).

"the President is always called 'the Old Man' by those who protect him, whether he is as old as Eisenhower or as young as Kennedy.": Ibid.

"a real character . . . Well, Fishbait, I warned them, and you sure didn't let me down.": Ibid.

"play an important role in the daily operation of the Senate.": U.S. Senate Page Program, pageprogram.senate.gov/page-program/.

"When the Speaker announced that [the amendment] had passed . . . I never saw such thundering applause. . . .": Letter by Albert Pillsbury (Senate page), 1865, from special exhibition at the U.S. Senate.

"We have a charming little boy about 12 years old . . . the same ceremony takes place again.": Letter by Rep. Thomas Hubbard, from special exhibition at the U.S. Senate.

"clearly the most magnificent high school campus in the world.": U.S. House of Representatives, History, Art & Archives, History of the House Page Program, "Schools, Dorms, & Reforms," history.house.gov/Exhibitions -and-Publications/Page-History/Historical-Essays/Schools/.

"I've been yearning for them to return . . . They really are part of the groups that make this place run.": Chris Cioffi, "Pages Are Back in the Senate after a Pandemic Hiatus," *Roll Call*, September 14, 2021.

"I'll never forget those four bells . . . It is a magnificent experience.": George Andrews III, "Last Day as a House Page," May 21, 2010, history.house.gov /Oral-History/People/George-W--Andrews-III/.

"It was the first time in my life I ever felt discriminated against as a woman, and it made me furious.": U.S. House of Representatives, History, Art & Archives, "Felda Looper, the First Female Page," history.house.gov/Historical -Highlights/1951-2000/Felda-Looper,-the-first-female-Page/.

"The practice of having only male pages in the House is a form of discrimination that should be ended.": Ibid.

"Somebody was going to be first. It was going to happen, and I was psyched it was me.": Ibid.

"The notion of—well, the work is too heavy or too hard . . . I can't believe they had you carry that.": Paulette Desell-Lund, interview by Kate Scott, April 15, 2014, www.senate.gov/about/women-of-the-senate/women-staff-oral -history-project.htm.

"I don't think I broke any barriers for anybody . . . so that there wouldn't be any hesitation.": U.S. House of Representatives, History, Art & Archives, History of the House Page Program, "Breaking Down Racial & Gender Barriers," history.house.gov/Exhibitions-and-Publications/Page-History/Historical -Essays/Barriers/.

"exceptional courage, attended by extraordinary decisiveness . . . life of any person or persons in actual imminent danger.": Code of Federal Regulations, Title 28, Chapter I, Part 50, §50.22.

"who has achieved outstanding or unusual recognition for character and service during a given calendar year.": Ibid.

"wandering among the people like discontented ghosts.": Alexander Hamilton, "The Federalist Papers: No. 72," March 21, 1788, avalon.law.yale.edu/18th _century/fed72.asp.

"There is nothing more pathetic in life than a former president.": Genevieve Carlton, "What Life Is Really Like for an Ex-President," *Chicago Tribune*, May 16, 2019, www.chicagotribune.com/2019/05/16/what-life-is-really -like-for-an-ex-president/.

"It was my intention to bury myself in complete retirement as much as any nun taking the veil.": John Quincy Adams, "John Quincy Adams Digital Diary," Primary Source Cooperative: Massachusetts Historical Society, March 6, 1829, www.primarysourcecoop.org/publications/jqa/document/jqadiaries -v36i-1829-03-p161--entry6.

"A life devoted to [ending slavery] would be nobly spent or sacrificed.": Louisa Thomas, "So Palpable a Stain: The Adams Family and Slavery in Washington, D.C.," *New Yorker*, April 25, 2016, www.newyorker.com/news/news-desk /so-palpable-a-stain-the-adams-family-and-slavery-in-washington-d-c.

"Have the colored people done anything . . . to justify it? No, sir.": Herbert C. Covey and Dwight Eisnach, eds., *Daily Life of African Americans in Primary Documents* (Bloomsbury Publishing, 2020).

"We shall overcome because the arc of the moral universe is long, but it bends toward justice.": Dr. Martin Luther King Jr., "Remaining Awake Through a Great Revolution" (speech, National Cathedral, Washington, D.C., March 31, 1968).

"I did all I could for the benefit of my needy and much imposed-upon people.": Eric Foner, "There Have Been 10 Black Senators Since Emancipation," *New York Times*, February 14, 2020.

"[Southern Democrats], sir, would not give . . . are not willing to grant it.": 2 Cong. Rec. 343–344 (1874).

"I can only raise my voice . . . my rights and in the interests of my oppressed people.": Office of the Historian and Office of the Clerk, *Black Americans in Congress, 1870–2022* (Washington, D.C.: U.S. Government Publishing Office, 2023), 55.

"This is not a Black story or a white story . . . of forward thinking.": Donaldson and Frear, "Meet Joseph Rainey, the First Black Congressman."

"We have public men who might well copy . . . Romualdo Pacheco.": U.S. House of Representatives, History, Art & Archives, "Pacheco, Romualdo," history .house.gov/People/Detail/19284.

"outside of the university atmosphere . . . were not wanted.": Tracy Conrad, "History: Desert Congressman Dalip Saund Was Democracy in Practice," *Desert Sun*, November 13, 2022, www.desertsun.com/story/life/2022/11/13 /palm-springs-history-dalip-saund-democracy-practice/10664196002/.

"Even though life for me did not seem very easy . . . various parts of the state as farmers.": Tom Patterson, "Triumph and Tragedy of Dalip Saund," *California Historian*, June 1992.

"than Massachusetts, Rhode Island, and Delaware combined": U.S. House of Representatives, History, Art & Archives, "Saund, Dalip Singh (Judge)," history.house.gov/People/Detail/21228.

"A woman's 'smoldering hope' . . . one of the most colorful Congressional contests of 1956": Gladwin Hill, "Colorful Contest Shaping on Coast," *New York Times*, December 27, 1955.

"Seldom if ever has the American melting pot . . . California's 29th Congressional

District": Conrad, "History: Desert Congressman Dalip Saund Was Democracy in Practice."

"To chronicle all his legislative achievements . . . for all Americans.": Office of the Historian and Office of the Clerk, *Asian and Pacific Islander Americans in Congress, 1900–2017* (Washington, D.C.: U.S. Government Publishing Office, 2017), 323.

"Calling 1992 the Year of the Woman . . . We're not a fad, a fancy, or a year.": U.S. Senate, "Year of the Woman," www.senate.gov/artandhistory/history /minute/year_of_the_woman.htm.

"I may be the first woman member of Congress, but I won't be the last.": Women and the American Story, "Life Story: Jeannette Rankin (1880–1973)," New York Historical Society, wams.nyhistory.org/modernizing-america/woman -suffrage/jeannette-rankin/.

"I saw that if we were to have . . . women would have to vote.": *American Masters*, "Jeannette Rankin: The First Woman Member of U.S. Congress," August 12, 2020, on PBS, www.pbs.org/wnet/americanmasters/jeannette-rankin -first-woman-member-us-congress-6r7oqu/15360/.

"I knew the women would stand by me . . . have been worth the effort": U.S. House of Representatives, History, Art & Archives, "Rankin, Jeannette," history.house.gov/People/Detail/20147.

"I am deeply conscious of . . . work cut out for me.": Ibid.

"You can no more win a war than you can win an earthquake": *American Masters*, "Jeannette Rankin: The First Woman Member of U.S. Congress," August 12, 2020, on PBS, www.pbs.org/wnet/americanmasters/jeannette-rankin -first-woman-member-us-congress-6r7oqu/15360/.

"I wish to stand for my country, but I cannot stand for war.": NCC Staff, "On This Day, Jeannette Rankin's History-Making Moment," *Constitution Daily* (blog), National Constitution Center, April 2, 2024, constitutioncenter.org /blog/on-this-day-jeanette-rankins-history-making-moment.

"As a woman, I can't go to war, and I refuse to send anyone else.": Ibid.

"The world must finally understand that we cannot settle disputes by eliminating human beings.": Glen Jeansonne and David Luhrssen, *A Time of Paradox: America from Awakening to Hiroshima, 1890–1945* (Lanham, MD: Rowman & Littlefield Publishers, Inc., 2007), 75.

"little lady from Arkansas": Nancy Hendricks, "Hattie Caraway, the First Woman Elected to the U.S. Senate, Faced a Familiar Struggle With Gender Politics," *Smithsonian*, January 2, 2020.

"If I can hold on to my sense . . . whether I get there or not.": Ibid.

"We have felt that we have not been consulted . . . ones in the past": Office of the

Historian and Office of the Clerk, *Asian and Pacific Islander Americans in Congress, 1900–2017*, 362.

"because there were only eight women . . . total population of women in the country.": Ibid, 361.

"an American hero, a leader and a trailblazer . . . fabric of our country.": Ibid, 363.

"I am the child of someone . . . change is going to happen.": "Mink!—My Mom Fought for Title IX, but It Almost Didn't Happen," directed by Ben Proudfoot, *Op-Docs*, June 23, 2022, *New York Times*, www.youtube.com /watch?v=faL6ERtj5oM.

"I have a way of talking that . . . You have to let them feel you.": U.S. House of Representatives, History, Art & Archives, "Chisholm, Shirley Anita," history.house.gov/People/Detail/10918.

"Actually, it's overdue, so I don't get terribly excited about it.": Walter Ray Watson, "A Look Back on Shirley Chisholm's Historic 1968 House Victory," NPR, November 6, 2018.

"There are a lot more veterans in my district than trees.": Featured Document Display: Congresswoman Shirley Chisholm: "Unbought and Unbossed," National Archives Museum, February 19–March 19, 2021, museum.archives .gov/featured-document-display-congresswoman-shirley-chisholm -unbought-and-unbossed.

"Shirley Chisholm's example transcends her life . . . Shirley Chisholm had guts.": Office of the Press Secretary, "Remarks by the President at Medal of Freedom Ceremony," November 24, 2015, obamawhitehouse.archives.gov /the-press-office/2015/11/24/remarks-president-medal-freedom-ceremony.

"I always felt a great sense of obligation . . . United States Congress.": U.S. House of Representatives, History, Art & Archives, "The Honorable Ileana Ros-Lehtinen," April 16, 2018, history.house.gov/Oral-History/Women /Representative-Ros-Lehtinen/.

"There was no epiphany. . . . but it's not about getting elected.": Daniella Silva, "Rep. Ileana Ros-Lehtinen, First Latina Woman Elected to Congress, Announces Retirement," NBC News, April 30, 2017.

"Power's not anything that anybody gives away. . . . fight for it.": Susan Page, "Nancy Pelosi's Birth 80 Years Ago Made Headlines, Too, as Perils Gathered for the Nation," *USA Today*, March 26, 2020.

"Nothing is more important than the full involvement of women . . . whatever that may be.": Nancy Pelosi, "Speaker Nancy Pelosi Shares Career Lessons and the Mentality That Keeps Her Going," Forbes, June 23, 2021, www .youtube.com/watch?v=RAqBW03iJNY.

"It's a historic moment for the Congress... anything is possible for them.": CBS News

Staff, "Nancy Pelosi Donates Suit, Gavel from Swearing In as First Woman House Speaker," CBS News, March 7, 2018, www.cbsnews.com/news/nancy-pelosi-donates-suit-gavel-from-swearing-in-as-first-woman-house-speaker/.

"Your path is your path, don't worry about following somebody else's path. It will have its own natural tempo.": Pelosi, "Speaker Nancy Pelosi Shares Career Lessons and the Mentality That Keeps Her Going."

"Freedom of speech . . . not exercised by others.": Lorraine Boissoneault, "The Senator Who Stood Up to Joseph McCarthy When No One Else Would," *Smithsonian*, September 13, 2018.

"I have few illusions and no money . . . you kind of like to try.": Hilary Rodham Clinton and Chelsea Clinton, *The Book of Gutsy Women: Favorite Stories of Courage and Resilience* (New York: Simon & Schuster, 2019), 33.

"She looked beyond the politics . . . all better for it.": George H. W. Bush, "Remarks at the Presentation Ceremony for the Presidential Medal of Freedom," American Presidency Project, July 6, 1989, www.presidency.ucsb.edu/documents/remarks-the-presentation-ceremony-for-the-presidential-medal-freedom.

"If you ask the direct question: 'Are you gay?' the answer is yes. So what?": AP Staff, "Representative Frank Discloses He Is Homosexual," Associated Press, May 31, 1987.

"I've said all along . . . I have anything to hide.": Ibid.

"For many years, I was ashamed . . . for my self-denial.": Barney Frank, "My Life as a Gay Congressman," *Politico*, March 12, 2015, www.politico.com/magazine/story/2015/03/barney-frank-life-as-gay-congressman-116027/.

"I should have come out a little earlier": Hugo Greenhalgh, "Gay President 20 Years Off, Says Former U.S. Congressman Barney Frank," Reuters, August 13, 2020.

"I don't want to leave the impression that I'm embarrassed about my life.": AP Staff, "Representative Frank Discloses He Is Homosexual."

"could make a difference . . . 'I could make a difference again.'": Matt Hrodey, "Tammy Baldwin's Long Game," *Milwaukee*, November 26, 2014.

"It shattered a glass ceiling that hadn't been shattered . . . Wisconsin to Congress.": Ibid.

"I really worried that I might . . . a very freeing moment.": Brooke Sopelsa, "Long Before the 'Rainbow Wave,' Sen. Tammy Baldwin Was Blazing a Trail," NBC News, December 20, 2018.

"Voters see immediately if you're authentic . . . integrity and honesty.": Ibid.

"substantive legislator": James Patterson, "Takano Fights Efforts to 'Turn Back Clock' on Equality," *Bay Area Reporter*, April 24, 2013, www.ebar.com

/story.php?ch=news&sc=&id=243495&title=takano_fights_efforts_to
_turn_back_clock_on_equality.

"More diversity in Congress will produce better outcomes.": Ibid.

"She was an example of . . . possibility for me.": Ana Marie Cox, "Mark Takano
Thinks Gay Men Can Learn from Jane Austen," *New York Times*, June
29, 2016.

"the birth" . . . "ambition.": Ibid.

"When Prop 8 passed in California . . . my inspiration for rethinking things.":
Linda Rapp, "Takano, Mark (b. 1970)," GLBTQ, 2012, www.glbtqarchive
.com/ssh/takano_mark_S.pdf.

"The significance of that achievement is . . . what it means to be vulnerable.":
Chris Johnson, "Takano on Path to Make History in Calif. Race: Democrat
Would Be First Out Gay Person of Color in Congress," *Washington Blade*,
December 22, 2011.

"I would never say that I speak for all Native people . . . legislation or policy.":
Jeffrey Masters, "Rep. Sharice Davids: Fighting for LGBTQ+, Native People
in Congress," *Advocate*, June 22, 2021.

"I've been very, very focused . . . tight budget.": Brian Ellison and Zach Perez,
"U.S. Rep. Sharice Davids on the Issues—Inflation, Abortion," *Shawnee
Mission Post*, September 14, 2022.

"I was homeless when I was a kid . . . and I stand before you today.": Rebekah L.
Sanders, "The Congresswoman Who Grew Up in a Gas Station," *Republic*,
September 29, 2017.

"Kyrsten was able to open the door . . . adult in teenager's clothing.": Ibid.

"They told me that I couldn't do it. . . . job and independence.": Ibid.

"We've made history, and we're proud of that . . . Congressional District.": Alyssa
Newcomb, "Kyrsten Sinema Becomes First Openly Bisexual Member of
Congress," ABC News, November 12, 2012.

"struggle of making it to the middle class": Ibid.

"I am so honored that Arizonans . . . time to get to work.": Tim Fitzsimons,
"Kyrsten Sinema Makes History as First Bisexual Member of U.S. Senate,"
NBC News, November 13, 2018.

"stubborn centrism": Jack Healy and Emily Cochrane, "Kyrsten Sinema Is at
the Center of It All. Some Arizonans Wish She Weren't," *New York Times*,
September 29, 2021.

"as he lay dying, [Lenthall] uttered a curse on the building that killed him.": Tim
Krepp, *Capitol Hill Haunts* (Charleston, SC: The History Press, 2012), 15.

"fixes its spectral eyes on its hapless victim . . . dark alleys.'": *Staunton Spectator
and Vindicator*, "Many Ghosts in Capitol—Demon Cats that Jump Over

Observer's Head," October 22, 1909.

"This demon cat emits a fierce yowl . . . over his head.": Ibid.

"When I shot at the critter it jumped right over my head.": Ibid.

"At about ten o'clock every night . . . empty corridors.": Hunter Spears, "'DC' Really Stands for Demon Cat . . . Which Haunts the U.S. Capitol," Boundary Stones, March 17, 2023, boundarystones.weta.org/2023/03/17 /dc-really-stands-demon-cat-which-haunts-us-capitol.

"The acoustic effects produced are astonishing": Ibid.

"It's quite possible that a cat walked across . . . 'That's the Demon Cat putting its initials there!'": Eric Grundhauser, "Why the U.S. Capitol's 'Demon Cat' Legend Is So Persistent," Atlas Obscura, March 13, 2018, www.atlasobscura .com/articles/is-there-a-demon-cat-in-the-us-capitol.

"in no condition for a physical contest . . . you had better be.": Robert Pohl, "Lost Capitol Hill: William Taulbee (Pt. 2)," The Hill Is Home, August 9, 2010, thehillishome.com/2010/08/lost-capitol-hill-william-taulbee-pt-2/#google _vignette.

"Can you see me now?": Peter Overby, "A Historic Killing in the Capitol Building," Morning Edition, NPR, February 19, 2007, www.npr.org /2007/02/19/7447550/a-historic-killing-in-the-capitol-building.

"The Sixth Regiment of Massachusetts . . . Vice President's Room his headquarters.": U.S. Senate, "The Civil War: The Senate's Story," www .senate.gov/artandhistory/history/common/civil_war/WarBegins.htm.

"You must never think of anything except the need, and how to meet it.": American Red Cross, "Clara Barton," www.redcross.org/about-us/who-we -are/history/clara-barton.html.

"One of the most curious and alarming . . . Statuary Hall at night.": Philadelphia Press, October 2, 1898, edited by Kathy Alexander/Legends of America, February 2024, www.legendsofamerica.com/ah-capitolghosts/.

"I had been to a part of the building where my duty takes me . . . anybody at all.": "Capitol Night Watchmen Tell Weird Ghost Stories," Washington Post, July 8, 1906.

"This is the last of the earth. I am content.": Troy Brownfield, "John Quincy Adams: America's Overachiever Gave the Presidency Pants," Saturday Evening Post, March 4, 2020, www.saturdayeveningpost.com/2020/03 /john-quincy-adams-americas-overachiever-gave-the-presidency-pants/.

"When they finally gave us a room . . . was haunted?": Krepp, Capitol Hill Haunts, 23.

"some of the older members . . . deliver it.": Emily Robinson, "The Congressional Bathtubs," Boundary Stones, January 24, 2018, boundarystones.weta

.org/2018/01/24/congressional-bathtubs.

"The man proceeds along the warm marble . . . never disturbed.": Ibid.

"Senate bathtub mystery": Ibid.

"killer tub": "Death of the Late Vice-President Henry Wilson, in the Vice-President's Room, at the Capitol, in Washington, D.C., on Wednesday Morning, November 22d," *Frank Leslie's Illustrated Newspaper*, December 11, 1875.

PERSPECTIVE

"Our kind friend, Mr. Carroll . . . for safe keeping.": "Dolley Madison to 'my Sister,' 23 August 1814," The Dolley Madison Project, Virginia Center for Digital History, www2.vcdh.virginia.edu/madison/exhibit/washington /letters/082314.html.

"All she carried off was the silver": Paul Jennings, *A Colored Man's Reminiscences of James Madison*, 1865, CreateSpace Independent Publishing Platform.

"When the British did arrive they ate up the very dinner . . . President's party.": Ibid.

"Then in that hour of deliverance and joyful triumph, my heart spoke.": Megan Smith, "You Asked, We Answer: Is the Star-Spangled Banner a Poem or a Song?", National Museum of American History, October 7, 2010, americanhistory.si.edu/explore/stories/you-asked-we-answer-star-spangled -banner-poem-or-song.

"With malice toward none; with charity for all . . . with all nations.": National Park Service, "Lincoln's Second Inaugural Address," www.nps.gov/linc /learn/historyculture/lincoln-second-inaugural.htm.

"The only thing we have to fear is fear itself.": National Park Service, "The Inauguration of Franklin D. Roosevelt," www.nps.gov/articles/000 /franklin-roosevelt-inauguration.htm.

"Those who say that we are in a time . . . where to look.": Colleen Shogan, "The Inaugural Address," White House Historical Association, November 18, 2020, www.whitehousehistory.org/the-inaugural-address.

"I don't want people to think I'm a windbag": Department of Education and Public Programs, John F. Kennedy Presidential Library and Museum, "Interpreting JFK's Inaugural Address," National Archives, www.jfklibrary .org/learn/education/teachers/curricular-resources/interpreting-jfks -inaugural-address.

"And so, my fellow Americans: ask not what your country can do for you . . . the freedom of man.": Department of Education and Public Programs, John F. Kennedy Presidential Library and Museum, "Ask Not What Your Country Can Do for You. . . ," National Archives, www.jfklibrary.org/learn/education

/teachers/curricular-resources/ask-not-what-your-country-can-do-for-you.

"If either the Capitol or the White House had been hit . . . to the country.":
Bill Sternberg, "What Was Flight 93's Target on 9/11?", *Washington Post*,
September 9, 2021.

"objective was to crash his airliner . . . White House.": Betsy Reed, "We've Got
Some Planes," *Guardian*, July 22, 2004.

"America is learning the names . . . the ones they loved.": Sara Rimer, "A Nation
Challenged: The Pennsylvania Crash; 44 Victims Are Remembered, and
Lauded," *New York Times*, September 18, 2001.

"We will never give up. . . . very disappointed in you.": Brian Naylor, "Read
Trump's Jan. 6 Speech, a Key Part of Impeachment Trial," NPR, February
10, 2021.

"My oath to support and defend the Constitution . . . which should not": Kat
Lonsdorf, Courtney Dorning, Amy Isakson, Mary Louise Kelly, and Ailsa
Chang, "A Timeline of How the Jan. 6 Attack Unfolded—Including Who
Said What and When," NPR, June 9, 2022.

"We fight like hell . . . country anymore.": Naylor, "Read Trump's Jan. 6 Speech,
a Key Part of Impeachment Trial."

"That's when it started hitting home": Author interview with Fred Johnson.

"When you're working in the kitchen . . . outside.": Ibid.

"One thing I remember . . . be calm.": Ibid.

"Are you traitors or are you with [Congress] or with us?": Interview with Cam
Sikurinec from January 6 Oral History Project, U.S. Capitol Historical Society.

"It was chaos from the crowd . . . Everything happened so fast.": Ibid.

"The first thing I remember seeing . . . other officers.": Ibid.

"Get down to the crypt! They're breaking down the door!": Ibid.

"a little nervous": Interview with Audra Jackson from January 6 Oral History
Project, U.S. Capitol Historical Society.

"They were beating on the door . . . seen us.": Ibid.

"We didn't know how bad it was.": Ibid.

"We just kept going . . . too scared.": Ibid.

"I was in staffer mode. . . . worse off.": Interview with Emma Kaplan from January
6 Oral History Project, U.S. Capitol Historical Society.

"They make this horrific whirring . . . it is loud.": Ibid.

"My mindset was, 'Let's get to work.' There was never any option but to go on.":
Ibid.

"They're almost to the Capitol!": Interview with Jordan Wilson from January 6
Oral History Project, U.S. Capitol Historical Society.

"I love this place . . . the space that I know.": Ibid.

"I had this mission of putting on the inauguration. . . . We didn't have time.":
Ibid.

"You could see the fright in their eyes . . . just scary.": Interview with Cam Sikurinec
from January 6 Oral History Project, U.S. Capitol Historical Society.

"Don't turn your First Amendment right into a criminal act.": Ibid.

"When the world is falling apart . . . sense of relief.": Author interview with Fred
Johnson.

"It's a room that I love so much . . . kind of condition.": Claire Wang, "Behind the
Viral Photo of Rep. Andy Kim Cleaning Up at Midnight After Riots," NBC
News, January 8, 2021.

"I feel blessed to have this opportunity . . . something extraordinary.": Ibid.

"like there should be some level of accountability . . . the House floor.": Interview
with Audra Jackson from January 6 Oral History Project, U.S. Capitol
Historical Society.

"It felt like a reason to stay.": Interview with Emma Kaplan from January 6 Oral
History Project, U.S. Capitol Historical Society.

EPILOGUE

"This is the American dream.": Martha Raddatz, "Bertie Bowman, Longest-
Serving Black Congressional Staffer in History, Dies at 92," *This Week*, ABC
News, October 29, 2023.

"Taught by the great example which . . . public duty.": *Dedication of the Washington
National Monument, Feb'y 21, 1885* (Washington, D.C.: Government
Printing Office, 1885), 13.

"A spot has been reserved within the walls . . . their country.": John Quincy Adams,
"First Annual Message," December 6, 1825, The American Presidency
Project, www.presidency.ucsb.edu/node/206789.

★ ★ ★

Image Credits

Grateful acknowledgment is given to the following sources for the images in this book:

p. 4: Photographs in the Carol M. Highsmith Archive, Library of Congress, Prints and Photographs Division; p. 21: Library of Congress, Serial and Government Publications Division; p. 23: Andrew W. Mellon Collection, courtesy of National Gallery of Art; p. 26: Library of Congress, Geography and Map Division; p. 27: Photo by Andrew J. Russell, Library of Congress, Prints and Photographs Division; p. 30 (both): Architect of the Capitol; p. 31: *The History of England, from the Earliest Periods, Volume 1* by Paul M. Rapin de Thoyras via Library of Congress; p. 32: Architect of the Capitol; p. 34: Architect of the Capitol; p. 35: U.S. Capitol Visitor Center; p. 36–37: Architect of the Capitol; p. 39: Architect of the Capitol; p. 46: George Grantham Bain Collection, Library of Congress, Prints and Photographs Division; p. 50–51: The Office of the Clerk, U.S. House of Representatives; p. 53: Photographs in the Carol M. Highsmith Archive, Library of Congress, Prints and Photographs Division; p. 57: Collection of the U.S. House of Representatives; p. 60: U.S. Senate, 111th Congress, Senate Photo Studio; p. 61: Architect of the Capitol; p. 63: George Mobley of The National Geographic, Library of Congress, Prints and Photographs Division; p. 64: *200 Notable Days: Senate Stories, 1787 to 2002—Chapter VII* by Richard A. Baker, Senate Historian; p. 65: Image courtesy of the U.S. House of Representatives Photography Office; p. 75: Architect of the Capitol via Flickr; p. 83: Photo by Benjamin Victor via Wikimedia Commons; p. 85: Nancy Pelosi, Sojourner Truth Bust Unveiling via Flickr; p. 88: Architect of the Capitol; p. 92: Architect of the Capitol via Flickr; p. 106: National Photo Company Collection, Library of Congress, Prints and Photographs Division; p.116 (from top): Brady-Handy photograph collection, Library of Congress, Prints and Photographs Division / Office of the Clerk, U.S. House of Representatives / Library of Congress Prints and Photographs Division; p. 117: Copy from the Fine Arts Library, Harvard University, by way of the Smithsonian Institution exhibition Votes for Women: A Portrait of Persistence; p. 122: Kate Andersen Brower; p. 125: Kate Andersen Brower; p. 132: Gian Panetta; p. 138: Photo by Harris & Ewing via Library of Congress, Prints and Photographs Division; p. 140: Photo by Douglas Graham via